# Embedded Computing Systems

Dr.C.S. Pillai

A. Latha

**Published by**

**Embedded Computing Systems**

**ISBN 978-93-86176-59-2**

**Author**

Dr.C.S. Pillai

A. Latha

**Bonfring**

309, 2nd Floor, 5th Street Extension, Gandhipuram,

Coimbatore-641 012.

Tamilnadu, India.

E-mail: info@bonfring.org

Website: www.bonfring.org

Phone: 0422 4213231

# Preface

The importance of **Embedded Computing Systems** is well known in various engineering fields. The book uses plain, lucid language to explain fundamental of this subject .This book provides logical method of explaining various complicated concepts and stepwise methods to explain the important topics.

Each chapter is well supported with necessary illustrations, practical examples and solved problems.

All care has been take care to make students comfortable in understanding the basic concepts of the subject.

We wish to express our thanks to all those who helped in making this book a reality.

We wish to thank the publisher and the entire team who have taken immense pain to get this book in time with quality printing.

*Dr.C.S. Pillai*
*A. Latha*

# Acknowledgement

# EMBEDDED COMPUTING SYSTEMS

Sub Code: 10CS72

Hrs/Week: 04

Total Hrs: 52

IA Marks :25

Exam Hours :03

Exam Marks :100

## Part–A

### UNIT – 1                                                6 Hours

**Embedded Computing:** Introduction, Complex Systems and Microprocessors, Embedded Systems Design Process, Formalism for System design, design Example: Model Train Controller.

### UNIT – 2                                                7 Hours

**Instruction Sets, CPUs:** Preliminaries, ARM Processor, Programming Input and Output, Supervisor mode, Exceptions, Traps, Coprocessors, Memory Systems Mechanisms, CPU Performance, CPU Power Consumption. Design Example: Data Compressor.

### UNIT – 3                                                6 Hours

**Bus-Based Computer Systems:** CPU Bus, Memory Devices, I/O devices, Component Interfacing, Designing with Microprocessor, Development and Debugging, System-Level Performance Analysis Design Example: Alarm Clock.

### UNIT – 4                                                7 Hours

**Program Design and Analysis:** Components for embedded programs, Models of programs, Assembly, Linking and Loading, Basic Compilation Techniques, Program optimization, Program-Level performance analysis, Software performance optimization, Program-Level energy and power analysis, Analysis and optimization of program size, Program validation and testing. Design Example: Software modem.

## Part–B

### UNIT – 5                                                6 Hours

**Real Time Operating System (RTOS) Based Design–1:** Basics of OS, Kernel, types of OSs, tasks, processes, Threads, Multitasking and Multiprocessing, Context switching, Scheduling Policies, Task Communication, Task Synchronization.

**UNIT – 6**                                                                                                    **6 Hours**

**RTOS-Based Design-2:** Inter process Communication mechanisms, Evaluating OS performance, Choice of RTOS, Power Optimization. Design Example: Telephone Answering machine

**UNIT – 7**                                                                                                    **7 Hours**

**Distributed Embedded Systems:** Distributed Network Architectures, Networks for Embedded Systems: I2C Bus, CAN Bus, SHARC Link Ports, Ethernet, Myrinet, Internet, Network Based Design. Design Example: Elevator Controller.

**UNIT – 8**                                                                                                    **7 Hours**

**Embedded Systems Development Environment:** The Integrated Development Environment, Types of File generated on Cross Compilation, Dis-assembler/Decompiler, Simulators, Emulators, and Debugging, Target Hardware Debugging.

## Text Books

1. Wayne Wolf: Computers as Components, Principles of Embedded Computing Systems Design, 2nd Edition, Elsevier, 2008.
2. Shibu K V: Introduction to Embedded Systems, Tata McGraw Hill, 2009 (Chapters 10, 13)

## Reference Books

1. James K. Peckol: Embedded Systems, A contemporary Design Tool, Wiley India, 2008
2. Tammy Neorgaard: Embedded Systems Architecture, Elsevier, 2005.

# Contents

# Unit-1

## Embedded Computing

## Complex Systems and Microprocessors

What is an embedded computer system? Loosely defined, it is any device that includes a programmable computer but is not itself intended to be a general-purpose computer. Thus, a PC is not itself an embedded computing system, although PCs are often used to build embedded computing systems. But a fax machine or a clock built from a microprocessor is an embedded computing system.

### *Embedding Computers*

A microprocessor is a single-chip CPU. Very large scale integration (VLSI) stet the acronym is the name technology has allowed us to put a complete CPU on a single chip since 1970s, but those CPUs were very simple. The first microprocessor-the Intel 4004, was designed for an embedded application, namely, a calculator. The calculator was not a general-purpose computer it merely provided basic arithmetic functions.

However, Ted Hoff of Intel realized that a general-purpose computer programmed properly could implement the required function, and that the computer-on-a-chip could then be reprogrammed for use in other products as well. Since integrated circuit design was (and still is) an expensive and time-consuming process, the ability to reuse the hardware design by changing the software was a key breakthrough. The HP-35 was the first handheld calculator to perform transcendental functions [Whi72]. It was introduced in 1972, so it used several chips to implement the CPU, rather than a single-chip microprocessor. How- ever, the ability to write programs to perform math rather than having to design digital circuits to perform operations like trigonometric functions was critical to the successful design of the calculator.

### *Characteristics of Embedded Computing Applications*

Embedded computing is in many ways much more demanding than the sort of programs that you may have written for PCs or workstations.

Functionality is important in both general-purpose computing and embedded computing, but embedded applications must meet many other constraints as well.

1) Complex algorithms: The operations performed by the microprocessor may be very sophisticated. For example, the microprocessor that controls an automobile engine

must perform complicated filtering functions to optimize the performance of the car while minimizing pollution and fuel utilization.

2) User interface: Microprocessors are frequently used to control complex user interfaces that may include multiple menus and many options. The moving maps in Global Positioning System (GPS) navigation are good examples of sophisticated user interfaces.

3) Real time: Many embedded computing systems have to perform in real time-if the data is not ready by a certain deadline, the system breaks. In some cases, failure to meet a deadline is unsafe and can even endanger lives. In other cases, missing a deadline does not create safety problems but does create unhappy customers-missed deadlines in printers, for example, can result in scrambled pages.

4) Multirate: Not only must operations be completed by deadlines, but many embedded computing systems have several real-time activities going on at the same time. They may simultaneously control some operations that run at slow rates and others that run at high rates. Multimedia applications are prime examples of multirate behavior. The audio and video portions of a multimedia stream run at very different rates, but they must remain closely synchronized. Failure to meet a deadline on either the audio or video portions spoils the perception of the entire presentation.

5) Manufacturing cost: The total cost of building the system is very important in many cases. Manufacturing cost is determined by many factors, including the type of microprocessor used, the amount of memory required, and the types of I/O devices.

6) Power and energy: Power consumption directly affects the cost of the hardware, since a larger power supply may be necessary. Energy con- sumption affects battery life, which is important in many applications, as well as heat consumption, which can be important even in desktop applications.

### *Why Use Microprocessors?*

1) There are many ways to design a digital system: custom logic, field programmable gate arrays (FPGAs), and so on. Why use microprocessors? There are two answers:

2) Microprocessors are a very efficient way to implement digital systems.

3) Microprocessors make it easier to design families of products that can be built to provide various feature sets at different price points and can be extended to provide new features to keep up with rapidly changing markets.

### The Physics of Software

Computing is a physical act. Although PCs have trained us to think about computers as purveyors of abstract information, those computers in fact do their work by moving electrons and doing work. This is the fundamental reason why programs take time to finish, why they consume energy, etc.

A prime subject of this book is what we might think of as the physics of software. Software performance and energy consumption are very important properties when we are connecting our embedded computers to the real world. We need to understand the sources of performance and power consumption if we are to be able to design programs that meet our application's goals.

Luckily, we don't have to optimize our programs by pushing around electrons. In many cases, we can make very high-level decisions about the structure of our programs to greatly improve their realtime performance and power consumption. As much as possible, we want to make computing abstractions work for us as we work on the physics of our software systems.

### Challenges in Embedded Computing System Design

External constraints are one important source of difficulty in embedded system design. Let's consider some important problems that must be taken into account in embedded system design.

### How much Hardware do we need?

We have a great deal of control over the amount of computing power we apply to our problem. We cannot only select the type of microprocessor used, but also select the amount of memory, the peripheral devices, and more. Since we often must meet both performance deadlines and manufacturing cost constraints, the choice of hardware is important—too little hardware and the system fails to meet its deadlines, too much hardware and it becomes too expensive.

### How do we Meet Deadlines?

The brute force way of meeting a deadline is to speed up the hardware so that the program runs faster. Of course, that makes the system more expensive.

It is also entirely possible that increasing the CPU clock rate may not make enough difference to execution time, since the program's speed may be limited by the memory system.

### *How do we Minimize Power Consumption?*

In battery-powered applications, power consumption is extremely important. Even in nonbattery applications, excessive power consumption can increase heat dissipation. One way to make a digital system consume less power is to make it un more slowly, but naively slowing down the system can obviously lead to missed deadlines. Careful design is required to slowdown the noncritical parts of the machine for power consumption while still meeting necessary performance goals.

### *How do we Design for Upgradability?*

The hardware platform may be used over several product generations, or for several different versions of a product in the same generation, with few or no changes. However, we want to be able to add features by changing software. How can we design a machine that will provide the required performance for software that we haven't yet written?

### *How Does it Really Work?*

Reliability is always important when selling products-customers rightly expect that products they buy will work. Reliability is especially important in some applications, such as safety-critical systems. If we wait until we have a running system and try to eliminate the bugs, we will be too late-we won't find enough bugs, it will be too expensive to fix them, and it will take too long as well. Another set of challenges comes from the characteristics of the components and systems them-selves. If workstation programming is like assembling a machine on a bench, then embedded system design is often more like working on a car—cramped, delicate, and difficult. Let's consider some ways in which the nature of embedded computing machines makes their design more difficult.

1) Complex testing: Exercising an embedded system is generally more difficult than typing in some data. We may have to run a real machine in order to generate the proper data. The timing of data is often important, meaning that we cannot separate the testing of an embedded computer from the machine in which it is embedded.

2) Limited observability and controllability: Embedded computing systems usually do not come with keyboards and screens. This makes it more difficult to see what is going on and to affect the system's operation. We may be forced to watch the values of electrical signals on the microprocessor bus, for example, to know what is going on inside the system. Moreover, in real-time applications we may not be able to easily stop the system to see what is going on inside.

3) Restricted development environments: The development environments for embedded systems (the tools used to develop software and hardware) are often much more limited than those available for PCs and workstations. We generally compile code on one type of machine, such as a PC, and download it onto the embedded system. To debug the code, we must usually rely on pro- grams that run on the PC or workstation and then look inside the embedded system.

### Performance in Embedded Computing

Embedded system designers, in contrast, have a very clear performance goal in mind-their program must meet its deadline. At the heart of embedded computing is real-time computing, which is the science and art of programming to deadlines. The program receives its input data; the deadline is the time at which a computation must be finished. If the program does not produce the required output by the deadline, then the program does not work, even if the output that it eventually produces is functionally correct.

1) CPU: The CPU clearly influences the behavior of the program, particularly when the CPU is a pipelined processor with a cache.

2) Platform: The platform includes the bus and I/O devices. The platform components that surround the CPU are responsible for feeding the CPU and can dramatically affect its performance.

3) Program: Programs are very large and the CPU sees only a small window of the program at a time. We must consider the structure of the entire program to determine its overall behavior.

4) Task: We generally run several programs simultaneously on a CPU, creating a multitasking system. The tasks interact with each other in ways that have profound implications for performance.

5) Multiprocessor: Many embedded systems have more than one processor-they may include multiple programmable CPUs as well as accelerators. Once again, the interaction between these processors adds yet more complexity to the analysis of overall system  performance.

## The Embedded System Design Process

A design methodology is important for three reasons.  First, it allows us to keep a scorecard on a design to ensure that we have done everything we need to do, such as optimizing performance or performing functional tests. Second, it allows us to develop computer-aided design tools. Developing a single program that takes in a concept for an embedded system and emits a completed design would be a daunting task, but by first breaking the process into manageable steps, we can work on automating (or at least semi automating) the steps one at a time. Third, a design methodology makes it much easier for members of a design team to communicate. By defining the overall process, team members can more easily understand what they are supposed to do, what they should receive from other team members at certain times, and what they are to hand off when they complete their assigned steps. Since most embedded systems are designed by teams, coordination is perhaps the most important role of a well-defined design methodology.

Specification, we create a more detailed description of what we want. But the specification states only how the system behaves, not how it is built. The details of the system's internals begin to take shape when we develop the architecture, which gives the system structure in terms of large components. Once we know the components we need, we can design those components, including both software modules and any specialized hardware we need. Based on those components, we can finally build a complete system.

In this section we will consider design from the top–down—we will begin with the most abstract description of the system and conclude with concrete details. The alternative is a bottom–up view in which we start with components to build a system. Bottom–up design steps are shown in the figure as dashed-line arrows. We need bottom–up design because we do not have perfect insight into how later stages of the design process will turn out. Decisions at one stage of design are based upon estimates of what will happen later: How fast can we make a particular function run? How much memory will we need? How much system bus capacity do we need? If our estimates are inadequate, we may have to backtrack and amend our original decisions to take the new facts into account. In general, the less experience we have with the design of similar systems, the more we will have to rely on bottom-up design information to help us refine the system. But the steps in the design process are only one axis along which we can view embedded system design. We also need to consider the major goals of the design:

1) Manufacturing cost.
2) Performance (both overall speed and deadlines) and
3) Power consumption.

We must also consider the tasks we need to perform at every step in the design process. At each step in the design, we add detail:

1) We must analyze the design at each step to determine how we can meet the specifications.
2) We must then refine the design to add detail.

3) And we must verify the design to ensure that it still meets all system goals, such as cost, speed, and so on.

## *Requirements*

Clearly, before we design a system, we must know what we are designing. The initial stages of the design process capture this information for use in creating the architecture and components. We generally proceed in two phases: First, we gather an informal description from the customers known as requirements, and we refine the requirements into a specification that contains enough information to begin designing the system architecture

1) Performance: The speed of the system is often a major consideration both for the usability of the system and for its ultimate cost. As we have noted, performance may be a combination of soft performance metrics such as approximate time to perform a user-level function and hard deadlines by which a particular operation must be completed.

2) Cost: The target cost or purchase price for the system is almost always a consideration. Cost typically has two major components: manufacturing cost includes the cost of components and assembly; nonrecurring engineering (NRE) costs include the personnel and other costs of designing the system.

3) Physical size and weight: The physical aspects of the final system can vary greatly depending upon the application. An industrial control system for an assembly line may be designed to fit into a standard-size rack with no strict limitations on weight. A handheld device typically has tight requirements on both size and weight that can ripple through the entire system design.

4) Power consumption: Power, of course, is important in battery-powered systems and is often important in other applications as well. Power can be specified in the requirements stage in terms of battery life-the customer is unlikely to be able to describe the allowable wattage.

Validating a set of requirements is ultimately a psychological task since it requires understanding both what people want and how they communicate those needs. One good way to refine at least the user interface portion of a system's requirements is to build a mock-up. The mock-up may use canned data to simulate functionality in a restricted demonstration, and it may be executed on a PC or a workstation. But it should give the customer a good idea of how the system will be used and how the user can react to it. Physical, nonfunctional models of devices can also give customers a better idea of characteristics such as size and weight. Shows a sample requirements form that can be filled out at the start of the project. We can use the form as a checklist in considering the basic characteristics of the system. Let's consider the entries in the form:

1) Name: This is simple but helpful. Giving a name to the project not only simplifies talking about it to other people but can also crystallize the purpose of the machine.

2) Purpose: This should be a brief one-or two-line description of what the system is supposed to do. If you can't describe the essence of your system in one or two lines, chances are that you don't understand it well enough.

3) Inputs and outputs: These two entries are more complex than they seem. The inputs and outputs to the system encompass a wealth of detail:

   - Types of data: Analog electronic signals? Digital data? Mechanical inputs?
   - Data characteristics: Periodically arriving data, such as digital audio samples? Occasional user inputs? How many bits per data element?
   - Types of I/O devices: Buttons? Analog/digital converters? Video displays?

4) Functions: This is a more detailed description of what the system does. A good way to approach this is to work from the inputs to the outputs: When the system receives an input, what does it do? How do user interface inputs affect these functions? How do different functions interact?

5) Performance: Many embedded computing systems spend at least some time controlling physical devices or processing data coming from the physical world. In most of these cases, the computations must be performed within a certain time frame. It is essential that the performance requirements be identified early since they must be carefully measured during implementation to ensure that the system works properly.

6) Manufacturing cost: This includes primarily the cost of the hardware components. Even if you don't know exactly how much you can afford to spend on system components, you should have some idea of the eventual cost range. Cost has a substantial influence on architecture: A machine that is meant to sell at $10 most likely has a very different internal structure than a $100 system.

7) Power: Similarly, you may have only a rough idea of how much power the system can consume, but a little information can go a long way. Typically, the most important decision is whether the machine will be battery powered or plugged into the wall. Battery-powered machines must be much more careful about how they spend energy.

8) Physical size and weight: You should give some indication of the physical size of the system to help guide certain architectural decisions. A desktop machine has much more flexibility in the components used than, for example, a lapel- mounted voice recorder.

A more thorough requirements analysis for a large system might use a form similar to Figure as a summary of the longer requirements document. After an introductory section containing this form, a longer requirements document could include details on each of the items mentioned in the introduction. For example, each individual feature described in the introduction in a single sentence may be described in detail in a section of the specification.

After writing the requirements, you should check them for internal consistency: Did you forget to assign a function to an input or output? Did you consider all the modes in which you want the system to operate? Did you place an unrealistic number of features into a battery-powered, low-cost machine?

To practice the capture of system requirements, Example 1.1 creates the requirements for a GPS moving map system.

### Example: 1.1 Requirements analysis of a GPS moving map

The moving map is a handheld device that displays for the user a map of the terrain around the user's current position; the map display changes as the user and the map device change position. The moving map obtains its position from the GPS, a satellite-based navigation system.

The moving map display might look something like the following figure.

1)  Functionality: This system is designed for highway driving and similar uses, not nautical or aviation uses that require more specialized databases and functions. The system should show major roads and other landmarks available in standard topographic databases.

2)  User interface: The screen should have at least 400 600 pixel resolution. The device should be controlled by no more than three buttons. A menu system should pop up on the screen when buttons are pressed to allow the user to make selections to control the system.

3)  Performance: The map should scroll smoothly. Upon power-up, a display should take no more than one second to appear, and the system should be able to verify its position and display the current map within 15 s.

4)  Cost: The selling cost (street price) of the unit should be no more than $100.

5)  Physical size and weight: The device should fit comfortably in the palm of the hand.

6)  Power consumption: The device should run for at least eight hours on four AA batteries.

### *Specification*

The specification is more precise—it serves as the contract between the customer and the architects. As such, the specification must be carefully written so that it accurately reflects the customer's requirements and does so in a way that can be clearly followed during design.

Specification is probably the least familiar phase of this methodology for neophyte designers, but it is essential to creating working systems with a minimum of designer effort. Designers who lack a clear idea of what they want to build when they begin typically make faulty assumptions early in the process that aren't obvious until they have a working system. At that point, the only solution is to take the machine apart, throw away some of it, and start again. Not only does this take a lot of extra time, the resulting system is also very likely to be inelegant, kludgey, and bug-ridden.

The specification should be understandable enough so that someone can verify that it meets system requirements and overall expectations of the customer. It should also be unambiguous enough that designers know what they need to build, Designers.

### *Architecture Design*

The specification does not say how the system does things, only what the system does. Describing how the system implements those functions is the purpose of the architecture.

The architecture is a plan for the overall structure of the system that will be used later to design the components that make up the architecture. The creation of the architecture is the first phase of what many designers think of as design.

To understand what an architectural description is, let's look at sample architecture for the moving map of Example 1.1. Figure shows sample system architecture in the form of a block diagram that shows major operations and data flows among them.

This block diagram is still quite abstract—we have not yet specified which operations will be performed by software running on a CPU, what will be done by special-purpose hardware, and so on.

The diagram does, however, go a long way toward describing how to implement the functions described in the specification. We clearly see, for example, that we need to search the topographic database and to render (i.e., draw) the results for the display. We have chosen to separate those functions so that we can potentially do them in parallel—performing rendering separately from searching the database may help us update the screen more fluidly.

### *Designing Hardware and Software Components*

The architectural description tells us what components we need. The component design effort builds those components in conformance to the architecture and specification. The components will in general include both hardware-FPGAs, boards, and so on—and software modules.

Some of the components will be ready-made. The CPU, for example, will be a standard component in almost all cases, as will memory chips and many other components. In the moving map, the GPS receiver is a good example of a specialized component that will nonetheless be a predesigned, standard component.

We can also make use of standard software modules. One good example is the topographic database. Standard topographic databases exist, and you probably want to use standard routines to access the database-not only is the data in a predefined format, but it is highly compressed to save storage. Using standard software for these access functions not only saves us design time, but it may give us a faster implementation for specialized functions such as the data decompression phase.

### *System Integration*

System integration is difficult because it usually uncovers problems. It is  often hard to observe the  system  in sufficient detail  to determine exactly what is wrong— the debugging facilities for embedded systems are usually much  more limited than what you would find on desktop systems. As a result, determining why things do not stet work correctly and how they can be fixed is a challenge in itself.

## Formalisms for System Design

As mentioned in the last section, we perform a number of different design tasks at different levels of abstraction throughout this book: creating requirements and specifications, architecting the system, designing code and designing tests. It is often helpful to conceptualize these tasks in diagrams.

Luckily, there is a visual language that can be used to capture all these   design tasks: the Unified Modeling Language (UML) [Boo99, Pil05].

UML was designed to be useful at many levels of abstraction in the design process. UML is useful because it encourages design by successive refinement and progressively adding detail to the design, rather than rethinking the design at each new level of abstraction.

UML is an object-oriented modeling language. We will see precisely what we mean by an object in just a moment, but object-oriented design emphasizes two concepts of importance:

1) It encourages the design to be described as a number of interacting objerather than a few large monolithic blocks of code

2) At least some of those objects will correspond to real pieces of software or hardware in the system. We can also use UML to model the outside world that interacts with our system, in which case the objects may correspond to people or other machines. It is sometimes important to implement something we think of at a high level as a single object using several distinct pieces of code or to otherwise break up the object correspondence in the implementations.

Object-oriented (often abbreviated OO) specification can be seen in two complementary ways:

1) Object-oriented specification allows a system to be described in a way that closely models real-world objects and their interactions.

2) Object-oriented specification provides a basic set of primitives that   can be used to describe systems with particular attributes, irrespective of the relationships of those systems' components to real-world objects.

Both views are useful.  At a minimum, object-oriented specification is a set of linguistic mechanisms.  In many cases, it is useful to describe a system in terms of real-world analogs. However, performance, cost, and so on may dictate that we change the  specification  to  be different in  some  ways from the real-world elements we are trying to  model  and  implement. In this case, the object-oriented specification mechanisms are still useful.

What is the relationship between an object-oriented specification and an object- oriented programming language (such as C++ [Str97])? A specification language may not be executable. But both object-oriented specification and programming languages provide similar basic methods for structuring large systems. Unified Modeling Language (UML)-the acronym is the name is a large language, and covering all of it is beyond the scope of this book. In this section, we introduce only a few basic concepts. In later chapters, as we need a few more UML concepts, we introduce them to the basic modeling elements introduced here. Because UML is so rich, there are many graphical elements in a UML diagram. It is important to be careful to use the correct drawing to describe something-for instance, UML distinguishes between arrows with open and filled-in arrowheads, and solid and broken lines. As you become more familiar with the language, uses of the graphical primitives will become more natural to you.

### *Structural Description*

By structural description, we mean the basic components of the system; we will learn how to describe how these components act in the next section. The principal component of an object-oriented design is, naturally enough, the object. An object includes a set of attributes that define its internal state. When implemented in a programming language, these attributes usually become variables or constants held in a data structure. In some cases, we will add the type of the attribute after A class is a form of type definition—all objects derived from the same class have the same characteristics, although their attributes may have different values. A class defines the attributes that an object may have. It also defines the operations that determine how the object interacts with the rest of the world. In a programming language, the operations would become pieces of code used to manipulate the object. The UML description of the Display class is shown in Figure 1.6. The class has the name that we saw used in the d1 object since d1 is an instance of class Display. The Display class defines the pixels attribute seen in the object; remember that when we instantiate the class an object, that object will have its own memory so that different objects of the same class have their own values for the attributes. Other classes can examine and modify class attributes; if we have to do something more complex than use the attribute directly, we define a behavior to perform that function.

A class defines both the interface for a particular type of object and that object's implementation. When we use an object, we do not directly manipulate its attributes—we can only read or modify the object's state through the operations that define the interface to the object. (The implementation includes both the attributes and whatever code is used to implement the operations.) As long as we do not change the behavior of the object seen at the interface, we can change the implementation as much as we want. This lets us improve the system by, for example, speeding up an operation or reducing the amount of memory required without requiring changes to anything else that uses the object. There are several types of relationships that can exist between objects and classes:

1) Association occurs between objects that communicate with each other but have no ownership relationship between them.
2) Aggregation describes a complex object made of smaller objects.
3) Composition is a type of aggregation in which the owner does not allow access to the component objects.
4) Generalization allows us to define one class in terms of another.

Unified Modeling Language, like most object-oriented languages, allows us to define one class in terms of another. An example is shown in Fig, where we derive two particular types of displays. The first, BW_display, describes a black- and-white display. This does not require us to add new attributes or operations, but we can specialize both to work on one-bit pixels. The second, Color_map_display, uses a graphic device known as a color map to allow the user to select from a behaviors—for example, large number of available colors even with a small number of bits per pixel. This class defines a color_map attribute that determines how pixel values are mapped onto display colors. A derived class inherits all the attributes and operations from its base class. In this class, Display is the base class for the two derived classes. A derived class is defined to include all the attributes of its base class. This relation is transitive—if Display were derived from another class,both BW_display and Color_map_display would inherit  all the attributes and operations of Display's base class as well. Inheritance has two purposes. It of course allows us to succinctly describe one class that shares some characteristics with another class. Even more important, it captures those relationships between classes and documents them. If we ever need to change any of the classes, knowledge of the class structure helps us determine the reach of changes—for example, should the change affect only Color_map_display objects or should it change all Display objects?

**Unified Modeling:** Language considers inheritance to be one form of general- ization. A generalization relationship is shown in a UML diagram as an arrow with an open (unfilled) arrowhead.  Both BW_display and Color versions of Display, so Display generalizes both of them.  UML also allows us to define multiple inheritance, in which a class is derived from more than one base class. (Most object-oriented programming languages support multiple inheritance as well.) An example of multiple inheritance is shown in Figure 1.8; we have omitted the details of the classes' attributes and operations for simplicity. In this case, we have created a Multimedia_display class by combining the Display class with a Speaker class for sound. The derived class inherits all the attributes and operations of both its base classes, Display and Speaker. Because multiple inheritance causes the sizes of the attribute set and operations to expand so quickly, it should be used with care.

A link describes a relationship between objects; association is to link as class is to object. We need links because objects often do not stand alone; associations let us capture type information about these links. examples of links and an association. When we consider the actual objects in the system, there is a set of messages that keeps track of the current number of active messages (two in this example) and points to the active messages. In this case, the link defines the contains relation. When generalized into classes, we define an association between the message set class and the message class. The association is drawn as a line between the two labeled with the name of the association, namely, contains. The ball and the number at the message class end indicate that the message message objects. Sometimes we may want to attach data to the links themselves; we can specify this in the association by attaching a class-like box to the association's edge, which holds the association's data. Typically, we find that we use a certain combination of elements in an object or class many times. We can give these patterns names, which are called stereotypes

## *Behavioral Description*

We have to specify the behavior of the system as well as its structure. One way to specify the behavior of an operation is a state machine. Figure shows UML states; the transition between two states is shown by a skeleton arrow. These state machines will not rely on the operation of a clock, as in hardware; rather, changes from one state to another are triggered by the occurrence of events.

1) A signal is an asynchronous occurrence. It is defined in UML by an object that is labeled as a <<signal>>. The object in the diagram serves as a declaration of the event's existence. Because it is an object, a signal may have parameters that are passed to the signal's receiver.

2) A call event follows the model of a procedure call in a programming language.

3) A time-out event causes the machine to leave a state after a certain amount of time. The label tm(time-value) on the edge gives the amount of time after which the transition occurs. A time-out is generally implemented with an external timer. This notation simplifies the specification and allows us to defer implementation details about the time-out mechanism.

We show the occurrence of all types of signals in a UML diagram in the same way—Let's consider a simple state machine specification to understand the semantics of UML state machines. A state machine for an operation of the display is shown in Figure. The start and stop states are special states that help us to organize the flow of the state machine. The states in the state machine represent different conceptual operations. In some cases, we take conditional transitions out of states based on inputs or the results of some computation done in the state. In other cases, we make an unconditional transition to the next state. Both the unconditional and conditional transitions make use of the call event. Splitting a complex operation into several states helps document the required steps, much as subroutines can be used to structure code. It is sometimes useful to show the sequence of operations over time, particularly when several objects are involved. In this case, we can create a sequence diagram, like the one for a mouse click scenario shown in Figure. A sequence diagram is somewhat similar to a hardware timing diagram, although the time flows vertically in a sequence diagram, whereas time typically flows horizontally in a timing diagram. The sequence diagram is designed to show a particular scenario or choice of events-it is not convenient for showing a number of mutually exclusive possibilities. In this case, the sequence shows what happens when a mouse click is on the menu region. Processing includes three objects shown at the top of the diagram. Extending below each object is its lifeline, a dashed line that shows how long the object is alive. In this case, all the objects remain alive for the entire sequence, but in other cases objects may be created or destroyed during processing. The boxes along the lifelines show the focus of control in the sequence, that is, when the object is actively processing. In this case, the mouse object is active only long enough to create the mouse_click event. The display object remains in play longer; it in turn uses call events to invoke the menu object twice: once to determine which menu item was selected and again to actually execute the menu call. The find_region( ) call is internal to the display object, so it does not appear as an event in the diagram.

## Model Train Controller

In order to learn how to use UML to model systems, we will specify a simple system, a model train controller, which is illustrated in Figure. The user sends messages to the train with a control box attached to the tracks. The control box may have familiar controls such as a throttle, emergency stop button, and so on. Since the train receives its electrical power from the two rails of the track, the control box can send signals to the train over the tracks by modulating the power supply voltage. As shown in the figure, the control panel sends packets over the tracks to the receiver on the train. The train includes analog electronics to sense the bits being transmitted and a control system to set the train motor's speed and direction based on those commands. Each packet includes an address so that the console can control several trains on the same track; the packet also includes an error correction code (ECC) to guard against transmission errors. This is a one-way communication system-the model train cannot send commands back to the user.

### *Requirements*

Before we can create a system specification, we have to understand the requirements. Here is a basic set of requirements for the system:

1) The console shall be able to control up to eight trains on a single track.
2) The speed of each train shall be controllable by a throttle to at least 63 different levels in each direction (forward and reverse).

There shall be an inertia control that shall allow the user to adjust the responsiveness of the train to commanded changes in speed. Higher inertia means that the train responds more slowly to a change in the throttle, simulating the inertia of a large train. The inertia control will provide at least eight different levels.

1) There shall be an emergency stop button.
2) An error detection scheme will be used to transmit messages.

| | |
|---|---|
| Name | Model train controller |
| Purpose | Control speed of up to eight model trains |
| Inputs | Throttle, inertia setting, emergency stop, train number |
| Outputs | Train control signals Set engine speed based upon inertia settings; respond to emergency stop |
| Performance | Can update train speed at least 10 times per second |
| Manufacturing cost | $50 |
| Power | 10 W (plugs into wall) |

size and weight Console should be comfortable for two hands, approximate size of standard keyboard; weight 2 pounds

We will develop our system using a widely used standard for model train control. We could develop our own train control system from scratch, but basing our system upon a standard has several advantages in this case: It reduces the amount of work we have to do and it allows us to use a wide variety of existing trains and other pieces of equipment.

## *DCC*

The **Digital Command Control (DCC)** standard (http://www.nmra.org/ standards/DCC/ standards_rps/DCCStds.html) was created by the National Model Railroad Association to support interoperable digitally-controlled model trains. Hob-byists started building homebrew digital control systems in the 1970s and Marklin developed its own digital control system in the 1980s. DCC was created to provide a standard that could be built by any manufacturer so that hobbyists could mix and match components from multiple vendors.

The DCC standard is given in two documents:

Standard S-9.1, the DCC Electrical Standard, defines how bits are encoded on the rails for transmission.

1) Standard S-9.2, the DCC Communication Standard, defines the packets that carry information Any DCC-conforming device must meet these specifications. DCC also provides several recommended practices. These are not strictly required but they provide some hints to manufacturers and users as to how to best use DCC.

The DCC standard does not specify many aspects of a DCC train system. It doesn't define the control panel, the type of microprocessor used, the programming language to be used, or many other aspects of a real model train system. The standard concentrates on those aspects of system design that are necessary for interoperability. Over standardization, or specifying elements that do not really need to be standardized, only makes the standard less attractive and harder to implement.

The Electrical Standard deals with voltages and currents on the track. While the electrical engineering aspects of this part of the specification are beyond the scope of the book, we will briefly discuss the data encoding here. The standard must be carefully designed because the main function of the track is to carry power to the locomotives. The signal encoding system should not interfere with power transmission either to DCC or non-DCC locomotives. A key requirement is that the data signal should not change the DC value of the rails.

The data signal swings between two voltages around the power supply volt- age. As shown in Figure, bits are encoded in the time between transitions, not by voltage levels. A 0 is at least 100 s while a 1is nominally 58 s. The durations of the high (above nominal voltage) and low (below nominal voltage) parts of a bit are equal to keep the DC value constant. The specification also gives the allowable variations in bit times that a conforming DCC receiver must be able to tolerate.

The standard also describes other electrical properties of the system, such as allowable transition times for signals. The DCC Communication Standard describes how bits are combined into packets and the meaning of some important packets. Some packet types are left undefined in the standard but typical uses are given in Recommended Practices documents.

1) P is the preamble, which is a sequence of at least 10 1 bits. The command station should send at least 14 of these 1 bits, some of which may be corrupted during transmission.

2) S is the packet start bit. It is a 0 bit.

3) A is an address data byte that gives the address of the unit, with the most significant bit of the address transmitted first. An address is eight bits long. The addresses 00000000, 11111110, and 11111111 are reserved.

4) s is the data byte start bit, which, like the packet start bit, is a 0.

5) D is the data byte, which includes eight bits. A data byte may contain an address, instruction, data, or error correction information.

6) E is a packet end bit, which is a 1bit.

A packet includes one or more data byte start bit/data byte combinations.

Note that the address data byte is a specific type of data byte.

A baseline packet is the minimum packet that must be accepted by all DCC implementations. More complex packets are given in a Recommended Practice document. A baseline packet has three data bytes: an address data byte that gives the intended receiver of the packet; the instruction data byte provides a basic instruction; and an error correction data byte is used to detect and correct transmission errors.

The instruction data byte carries several pieces of information. Bits 0–3 provide a 4-bit speed value. Bit 4 has an additional speed bit, which is interpreted as the least significant speed bit. Bit 5 gives direction, with 1 for forward and 0 for reverse. Bits 7–8 are set at 01 to indicate that this instruction provides speed and direction.

The error correction databyte is the bitwise exclusive OR of the address and instruction data bytes.

The standard says that the command unit should send packets frequently since a packet may be corrupted. Packets should be separated by at least 5 ms.

### *Conceptual Specification*

Digital Command Control specifies some important aspects of the system, particularly those that allow equipment to interoperate. But DCC deliberately does not specify everything about a model train control system. We need to round out our specification with details that complement the DCC spec. A conceptual specification allows us to understand the system a little better. We will use the experience gained by writing the conceptual specification to help us write a detailed specification to be given to a system architect. This specification does not correspond to what any commercial DCC controllers do, but it is simple enough to allow us to cover some basic concepts in system design.

A train control system turns commands into packets. A command comes from the command unit while a packet is transmitted over the rails. Commands and packets may not be generated in a 1-to-1 ratio. In fact, the DCC standard says that command units should resend packets in case a packet is dropped during transmission.

We now need to model the train control system itself. There are clearly two major subsystems: the command unit and the train-board component as shown in Figure 1.16. Each of these subsystems has its own internal structure. The basic relationship between them is illustrated in Figure. This figure shows a UML collaboration diagram; we could have used another type of figure, such as a class or object diagram, but we wanted to emphasize the transmit/receive relationship between these major subsystems. The command unit and receiver are each represented by objects; the command unit sends a sequence of packets to the train's receiver, as illustrated by the arrow. The notation on the arrow provides both the type of message sent and its sequence in a flow of messages; since the console sends all the messages, we have numbered the arrow's messages as 1..n. Those messages are of course carried over the track. Since the track is not a computer component and is purely passive, it does not appear in the diagram. However, it would be perfectly legitimate to model the track in the collaboration diagram, and in some situations it may be wise to model such nontraditional components in the specification diagrams. For example, if we are worried about what happens when the track breaks,

1.  Knobs* describes the actual analog knobs, buttons, and levers on the control panel.

    - Sender* describes the analog electronics that send bits along the track.

Likewise, the Train makes use of three other classes that define its components:

2.  The Receiver class knows how to turn the analog signals on the track into digital form.

3.  The Controller class includes behaviors that interpret the commands and figures out how to control the motor.

4.  The Motor interface class defines how to generate the analog signals required to control the motor.

We define two classes to represent analog components:

- Detector* detects analog signals on the track and converts them into digital form.

- Pulser* turns digital commands into the analog signals required to control the motor speed.

## Instruction Set CPUs

Harvard architectures are widely used today for one very simple reason-the separation of program and data memories provides higher performance for digital signal processing. Processing signals in real-time places great strains on the data access system in two ways: First, large amounts of data flow through the CPU; and second, that data must be processed at precise intervals, not just when the CPU gets around to it. Data sets that arrive continuously and periodically are called *streaming data*. Having two memories with separate ports provides higher memory band-width; not making data and memory compete for the same port also makes it easier to move the data at the proper times. DSPs constitute a large fraction of all micro- processors sold today, and most of them are Harvard architectures. A single example shows the importance of DSP: Most of the telephone calls in the world go through at least two DSPs, one at each end of the phone call.

Another axis along which we can organize computer architectures relates to their instructions and how they are executed. Many early computer architectures were what is known today as *complex instruction set computers (CISC)*. These machines provided a variety of instructions that may perform very complex tasks, such as string searching; they also generally used a number of different instruction formats of varying lengths. One of the advances in the development of high-performance microprocessors was the concept of *reduced instruction set computers (RISC)*. These computers tended to provide somewhat fewer and simpler instructions. The instructions were also chosen so that they could be efficiently executed in *pipelined* processors. Early RISC designs substantially outperformed CISC designs of the period. As it turns out, we can use RISC techniques to efficiently execute at least a common subset of CISC instruction sets, so the performance gap between RISC-like and CISC-like instruction sets has narrowed somewhat. Beyond the basic RISC/CISC characterization, we can classify computers by several characteristics of their instruction sets. The instruction set of the computer defines the interface between software modules and the underlying hardware; the instructions define what the hardware will do under certain circumstances. Instructions can have a variety of characteristics, including:

- Fixed versus variable length.
- Addressing modes.
- Numbers of operands.
- Types of operations supported.

The set of registers available for use by programs is called the programming model, also known as the programmer model. (The CPU has many other registers that are used for internal operations and are unavailable to programmers.) There may be several different implementations of an architecture. In fact, the architecture definition serves to define those characteristics that must be true of all implementations and what may vary from implementation to implementation. Different CPUs may offer different clock speeds, different cache configurations, changes to the bus or interrupt lines, and many other changes that can make one model of CPU more attractive than another for any given application.

### Assembly Language

Figure shows a fragment of ARM assembly code to remind us of the basic features of assembly languages. Assembly languages usually share the same basic features:

1) One instruction appears per line.
2) Labels, which give names to memory locations, start in the first column.
3) Instructions must start in the second column or after to distinguish them from labels.
4) Comments run from some designated comment character (in the case of ARM) to the end of the line.

Assembly language follows this relatively structured form to make it easy for the assembler to parse the program and to consider most aspects of the program line by line. (It should be remembered that early assemblers were written in assembly language to fit in a very small amount of memory. Those early restrictions have carried into modern assembly languages by tradition). Figure shows the format of an ARM data processing instruction such as an ADD. For the instruction ADDGT r0,r3,#5 the cond field would be set according to the GT condition (1100), the opcode field would be set to the binary code for the ADD instruction (0100), the first operand register Rn would be set to 3 to represent r3, the destination register Rd would be set to 0 for r0, and the operand 2 field would be set to the immediate value of 5. Assemblers must also provide some pseudo-ops to help programmers create complete assembly language programs. An example of a pseudo-op is one that allows data values to be loaded into memory locations. These allow constants, for example, to be set into memory. An example of a memory allocation pseudo-op for ARM is shown in Figure 2.5. The ARM % pseudo-op allocates a block of memory of the size specified by the operand and initializes those locations to zero.

```
label1ADR r4,c
LDR r0,[r4]; a comment
ADR r4,d LDR r1,[r4]
```

SUB r0,r0,r1; another comment

An example of ARM assembly language

## Processor and Memory Organization

Different versions of the ARM architecture are identified by different numbers. ARM7 is a von Neumann architecture machine, while ARM9 uses a Harvard architecture. However, this difference is invisible to the assembly language programmer, except for possible performance differences. The ARM architecture supports two basic types of data:

1) The standard ARM word is 32 bits long.

2) The word may be divided into four 8-bit bytes.

ARM7 allows addresses up to 32 bits long. An address refers to a byte, not word. Therefore, the word 0 in the ARM address space is at location 0, the word 1 is at 4, the word 2 is at 8, and so on. (As a result, the PC is incremented by 4 in the absence of a branch.) The ARM processor can be configured at power-up to address the bytes in a word in either little-endian mode (with the lowest-order byte residing in the low-order bits of the word) or big-endian mode (the lowest-order byte stored in the highest bits of the word), as illustrated in Figure [Coh81].

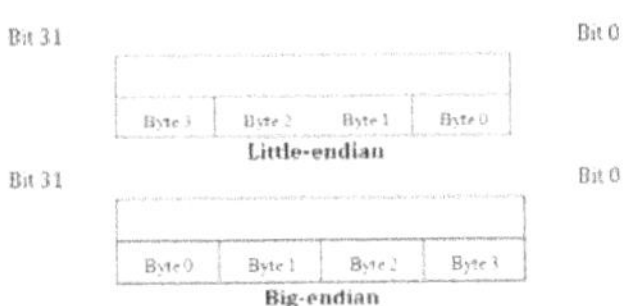


Byte organizations within an ARM word.

## Data Operations

Arithmetic and logical operations in C are performed in variables. Variables are implemented as memory locations. Therefore, to be able to write instructions to perform C expressions and assignments, we must consider both arithmetic and logical instructions as well as instructions for reading and writing memory. Below Figure shows a sample fragment of C code with data declarations and several assignment statements. The variables a, b, c, x, y, and z all become data locations in memory. In most cases data are kept relatively separate from instructions in the program's memory image. In the ARM processor, arithmetic and logical operations cannot be performed directly on memory locations. While some processors allow such operations to directly reference main memory, ARM is a load-store architecture—data operands must first be loaded into the CPU and then stored back to main memory to save the results. Figure 2.8 shows the registers in the basic ARM programming model. ARM has 16 general-purpose registers, r0 through r15. Except for r15, they are identical—any operation that can be done on one of them can be done on the other one also. The r15 register has the same capabilities as the other registers, but it is also used as the program counter. The program counter should of course not be overwritten for use in data operations. However, giving the PC the properties of a general-purpose register allows the program counter value to be used as an operand in computations, which can make certain programming tasks easier. The other important basic register in the programming model is the current program status register(CPSR). This register is set automatically during every arithmetic, logical, or shifting operation. The top four bits of the CPSR hold the following useful information about the results of that arithmetic/logical operation:

1) The negative (N) bit is set when the result is negative in two's-complement arithmetic.

2) The zero (Z) bit is set when every bit of the result is zero.

3) The carry (C) bit is set when there is a carry out of the operation.

4) The overflow (V)bit is set when an arithmetic operation results in an overflow.

$$\text{int a, b, c, x, y, z;}$$
$$x(ab)c;$$
$$ya*(bc);$$
$$z(a << 2) \mid (b \ \& \ 15);$$

A C fragment with data operations.

These bits can be used to check easily the results of an arithmetic operation. However, if a chain of arithmetic or logical operations is performed and the inter- mediate states of the CPSR bits are important, then they must be checked at each step since the next operation changes the CPSR values. Example 2.1 illustrates the computation of CPSR bits.

### *Example 2.1*

### *Status bit Computation in the ARM*

An ARM word is 32 bits. In C notation, a hexadecimal number starts with 0x, such as 0xffffffff, which is a two's-complement representation of  1 in a 32-bit  word. Here are some sample calculations:

- *1 1 0:* Written in 32-bit format, this becomes 0xffffffff 0x10x0, giving the CPSR value of NZCV 1001.
- *0 1 1:* 0x0 0x1 0xffffffff, with NZCV 1000.

- $2^{31}$ $1$ $1$ $2^{31}$ :0x7ffffff  0x1 0x80000000, with NZCV 1001.

The basic form of a data instruction is simple:

ADD r0,r1,r2

This instruction sets register r0 to the sum of the values stored in r1 and r2. In addition to specifying registers as sources for operands, instructions may also provide *immediate operands*, which encode a constant value directly in the instruction. For example,

ADD r0,r1,#2

sets r0 to r1  2.

The major data operations are summarized in Figure 2.9.  The arithmetic operations perform addition and subtraction; the with-carry versions include the current value of the carry bit in the computation. RSB performs a subtraction with the order of the two operands reversed, so that RSB r0, r1, r2 sets r0 to be r2 r1. The bit-wise logical  operations perform logical AND, OR, and XOR operations (the exclusive or is called EOR). The BIC instruction stands for bit clear: BIC r0, r1, r2 sets r0 to r1 and not r2. This instruction uses  the  second source operand as a mask:Where a bit in the mask is 1, the corresponding bit in the first source operand is cleared. The MUL instruction multiplies two values, but with some restrictions:  No operand may be an immediate, and the two source operands must be different registers. The MLA instruction performs a multiply-accumulate operation, particularly useful in matrix operations and  signal  processing.  The instruction

MLA r0,r1,r2,r3

sets r0 to the value r1 r2 r3.

The shift operations are not separate instructions—rather, shifts can be applied to arithmetic and logical instructions. The shift modifier is always applied to the second source operand. A left shift moves bits up toward the most-significant bits, while a right  shift moves  bits down  to the least-significant bit in the word. The LSL and LSR modifiers perform left and right logical shifts, filling the least-significant bits of the operand with zeroes. The arithmetic shift left is equivalent to an LSL, but the ASR copies the sign bit— if the sign is 0, a 0 is copied, while if the sign is 1, a

1 is copied. The rotate modifiers always rotate right, moving the bits that fall off the least-significant bit up to the most-significant bit in the word. The RRX modifier performs a 33-bit rotate, with the CPSR's C bit being inserted above the sign bit of the word; this allows the carry bit to be included in the rotation. Stored in the register is used as the address to  be fetched

from memory; the result of that fetch is the desired operand value. Thus, as illustrated in Figure 2.13, if we set r1

0    100, the instruction

LDR r0,[r1]

sets r0 to the value of memory location 0x100. Similarly, STR r0,[r1] would store the contents of r0 in the memory location whose address is given in r1. There are several possible variations:

LDR r0,[r1, – r2]

This step. Thus, as shown in Figure 2.14, if we give location 0x100 the name FOO, we can use the pseudo-operation to perform the same function of loading r1 with the address  0x100.

ADR r1,FOO

Example 2.2 illustrates how to implement C assignments in ARM  instruction.

### *Example 2.2*

### *C assignments in ARM instructions*

We will use the assignments of Figure 2.7. The semicolon (;) begins a comment after an instruction, which continues to the end of that line. The statement

$$x \quad (a \quad b) \quad c;$$

can be implemented by using r0 for $a$, r1 for $b$, r2 for  $c$ , and r3 for $x$ . We also need registers for indirect addressing.  In this case, we will reuse the same indirect addressing register, r4, for each variable load. The code must load the values of $a$, $b$, and $c$ into these registers before performing the arithmetic, and it must store the value of $x$ back to memory when it is done. This code performs the following necessary steps:

ADR r4,a      ; get address for a LDR r0,[r4] ; get value of a

ADR r4,b      ; get address for  b,

reusing r4

LDR r1,[r4] ; load  value  of b

ADD r3,r0,r1 ; set intermediate result  for x to a + b

ADR r4,c      ; get address for c LDR r2,[r4] ; get value of c

SUB r3,r3,r2 ; complete computation of ADR r4,x; get address for  x

STR r3,[r4] ; store x at proper LDR r0,[r4] ; get value of a

MUL r2,r2,r0 ; compute final value of ADR r4,y ; get address for y

STR r2,[r4] ; store value of y at proper location

## *Flow of Control*

The B (branch) instruction is the basic mechanism in ARM for changing the flow of control. The address that is the destination of the branch is often called the branch target.

Branches are PC-relative—the branch specifies the offset from the current PC value to the branch target.

The offset is in words, but because the ARM is byte-addressable, the offset is multiplied by four (shifted left two bits, actually) to form a byte address. Thus, the instruction:

B #100

will add 400 to the current PC value.

We often wish to branch conditionally, based on the result of a given computation. The if statement is a common example.

The ARM allows any instruction, including branches, to be executed conditionally. This allows branches to be conditional, as well as data operations.

Figure 2.15 summarizes the condition codes.

## *Example 2.3*

## *Implementing an if statement in ARM*

We will use the following if statement as an example:

if (a < b) { x = 5;

y = c + d;

}

lse x = c – d;

The implementation uses two blocks of code, one for the true case and another for the false case. A branch may either fall through to the true case or branch to the false case:

, compute and test the condition A

DR r4,a ; get address for a

```
        LDR r0,[r4]    ; get value of a
        ADR r4,b       ; get address for b
        LDR r1,[r4]    ; get value of b
        CMP r0, r1     ; compare a < b
        BGE fblock     ; if a >= b, take branch
        ; the true block follows
        MOV r0,#5      ; generate value for x
        ADR r4,x       ; get address for x
        STR r0,[r4]    ; store value of x
        ADR r4,c; get address for c
        LDR r0,[r4]; get value of c
        ADR r4,d       ; get address for d
        LDR r1,[r4]    ; get value of d
        ADD r0,r0,r1 ; compute c + d
        ADR r4,y       ; get address for y
        STR r0,[r4]    ; store value of y B after ; branch around the false   block ;
        the false block follows
        fblock ADR r4,c ; get address
        for c
        LDR r0,[r4]    ; get value of c
        ADR r4,d       ; get address for d
        LDR r1,[r4]    ; get value of d
        SUB r0,r0,r1 ; compute c - d
        ADR r4,x       ; get address for x
        STR r0,[r4]    ; store   value of x after ... ; code after the if statement
```

## Example 2.4

### Implementing the C switch statement in ARM

The switch statement in C takes the following form:

switch (test) { case 0: ... break; case 1: ... break;

...

}

The above statement could be coded like an if statement by first testing test A, then test B, and so forth.

However, it can be more efficiently implemented by using base- plus-offset addressing and building what is known as a **branch table:**

ADR r2,test ; get address for test

LDR r0,[r2] ; load value for test

ADR r1,switchtab ; load address for

switch table

LDR r15,[r1,r0,LSL  #2]

switchtab DCD case0 DCD case1

...

case0            ... ; code for  case 0

...

case1            ... ; code for  case 1

...

This implementation uses the value of test as an offset into a table, where the table holds the addresses for the blocks of code that implement the various cases.

The heart of this code is the LDR instruction, which packs a lot of functionality into a single instruction:

1)   It shifts the value of r0 left two bits to turn the offset into a word address.
2)   It uses base plus offset addressing to add the left-shifted value of test (held in r0) to the address of the base of the table held in r1.

3) It sets the PC (r15) to the new address computed by the instruction. The loop is a very common C statement, particularly in signal processing code. Loops can be naturally implemented using conditional branches. Because addressing mode. A simple but common use of a loop is in the FIR filter, which is explained in Application Example 2.1; the loop-based implementation of the FIR filter is described in Example 2.5.

## Application Example 2.1

### FIR filters

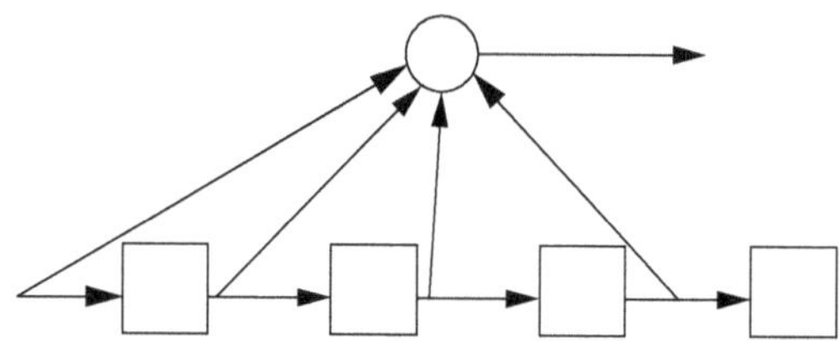

A *finite impulse response (FIR) filter* is a  commonly  used  method for processing signals; we make use of it in Section 5.11. The FIR filter is a simple sum  of products:

## Example 2.5

### An FIR filter for the ARM

The C code for the FIR filter of Application Example 2.1 follows:

```
for (i = 0, f = 0; i < N; i++)

f = f + c[i] * x[i];
```

We can address the arrays $c$ and $x$ using base-plus- offset addressing: We will load one register with the address of the zeroth element of each array and use the register holding $i$ as the offset.

The C language [Ker88] defines a for loop as equivalent to a while loop with proper initialization and termination.  Using that rule, the for loop can be rewritten  as

```
i = 0;

f = 0;

while (i < N) {

f = f + c[i]*x[i]; i++;

}
```

Here is the code for the loop:

```
; loop initiation code
MOV r0,#0    ; use r0 for i, set to 0
MOV r8,#0    ; use a separate index for arrays
ADR r2,N      ; get address for N
LDR r1,[r2] ; get value of N for loop termination test
MOV r2,#0    ; use r2 for f, set to 0
ADR r3,c       ; load r3 with address of base of c array
ADR r5,x       ; load r5 with address of base of x array
; loop body
loop LDR r4,[r3,r8] ; get value of c[i] LDR r6,[r5,r8] ; get value of x[i] MUL r4,r4,r6      ; compute c[i]*x[i]
ADD r2,r2,r4 ; add into running sum f
; update loop counter and array index
ADD r8,r8,#4; add one word offset to array index
ADD r0,r0,#1; add 1 to i
; test for exit CMP r0,r1
BLT loop; if i < N, continue loop loopend...
```

The other important class of C statement to consider is the **function**. A C function returns a value (unless its return type is void); **subroutine** or **procedure** are the common names for such a construct when it does not return a value. Consider this simple use of a function in C:

```
x = a + b;
foo(x);
y = c - d;
```

A function returns to the code immediately after the function call, in this case the assignment to y. A simple branch is insufficient because we would not know where to return. To properly return, we must save the PC value when the procedure/function is called and, when the procedure is finished, set the PC to the address of the instruction just after the call to the procedure. (You don't want to endlessly execute the procedure, after all.) The branch-and-link instruction is used in the ARM for procedure calls. For instance,

BL foo

Will perform a branch and link to the code starting at location foo (using PC-relative addressing, of course). The branch and link is much like a branch, except that before branching it stores the current PC value in r14. Thus, to return from a procedure, you simply move the value of r14 to r15:

MOV r15, r14

You should not, of course, overwrite the PC value stored in r14 during the procedure.

The C code shows a series of functions that call other functions: f1( ) calls f2( ), which in turn calls f3( ). The right side of the figure shows the state of the procedure call stack during the execution of f3( ). The stack contains one activation record for each active procedure. When f3( ) finishes, it can pop the top of the stack to get its return address, leaving the return address for f2( ) waiting at the top of the stack for its return. We can also use the procedure call stack to pass parameters. The conventions used to pass values into and out of procedures is known as procedure linkage. To pass parameters into a procedure, the values can be pushed onto the stack just before the procedure call. Once the procedure returns, those values must be popped off the stack by the caller, since they may hide a return address or other useful information on the stack.

Example 2.6 illustrates the programming of a simple C function.

### Example 2.6

### Procedure calls in ARM

We use as an example one of the functions from Figure 2.16:

void f1(inta) {

f2(a);

}

Here is some handwritten code for

f1(), which includes a call to f2(): f1  LDR r0,[r13];  load  value of a argument into r0 from stack

; call f2()

STR r14,[r13]! ; store f1's return address on the stack

STR r0,[r13!] ; store argument to f2 onto stack

BL f2            ; branch and link to f2

; return from f1()

SUB r13,#4   ; pop f2's argument off the

stack

LDR r13!,r15 ; restore registers and

return

We use base-plus-offset addressing to load the value passed into f1() into a register for use by r1. To call f2(), we first push f1()'s return address, stored in r14 by the branch-and-link instruction executed to get into f1(), onto the stack. We then push f2()'s parameter onto the stack. In both cases, we use auto increment addressing to both store onto the stack and adjust the stack pointer. To return, we must first adjust the stack to get rid of f2()'s parameter that hidesreturn address; we then use autoincrement addressing to pop f1()'s return address off the stack and into the PC (r15).

## Programming Input and Output

The basic techniques for I/O programming can be understood relatively independent of the instruction set. In this section, we cover the basics of I/O programming and place them in the contexts of both the ARM and C55x. We begin by discussing the basic characteristics of I/O devices so that we can understand the requirements they place on programs that communicate with them.

### 1) Input and Output Devices

Input and output devices usually have some analog or nonelectronic component-for instance, a disk drive has a rotating disk and analog read/write electronics. But the digital logic in the device that is most closely connected to the CPU very strongly resembles the logic you would expect in any computer system.

Figure 3.1 shows the structure of a typical I/O device and its relationship to the CPU. The interface between the CPU and the device's internals (e.g.,the rotating disk and read/write electronics in a disk drive) is a set of registers. The CPU talks to the device by reading and writing the registers. Devices typically have several registers:

1. Data registers hold values that are treated as data by the device, such as the data read or written by a disk.

2. Status registers provide information about the device's operation, such as whether the current transaction has completed.

### *Application Example 3.1*

### *The 8251 UART*

The 8251 **UART** (Universal Asynchronous Receiver/Transmitter) [Int82] is the original device used for serial communications, such as the serial port connections on PCs. The 8251 was introduced as a stand-alone integrated circuit for early microprocessors. Today, its functions are typically subsumed by a larger chip, but these more advanced devices still use the basic programming interface defined by the 8251. The UART is programmable for a variety of transmission and reception parameters. However, the basic format of transmission is simple. Data are transmitted as streams of characters, each of which has the following form:

Every character starts with a start bit (a 0) and a stop bit (a 1). The start bit allows the receiver to recognize the start of a new character; the stop bit ensures that there will be a transition at the start of the stop bit. The data bits are sent as high and low voltages at a uniform rate. That rate is known as the ***baud rate*** ; the period of one bit is the inverse of the baud rate.

Before transmitting or receiving data, the CPU must set the UART's mode registers to correspond to the data line's characteristics. The parameters for the serial port are familiar from the parameters for a serial communications program (such as Kermit):

1. the baud rate;
2. the number of bits per character (5 through 8);
3. whether parity is to be included and whether it is even or odd; and
4. the length of a stop bit (1, 1.5, or 2 bits).

The UART includes one 8-bit register that buffers characters between the UART and the CPU bus.

The Transmitter Ready output indicates that the transmitter is ready to accept a data character; the Transmitter Empty signal goes high when the UART has no characters to send. On the receiver side, the Receiver Ready pin goes high when the UART has a character ready to be read by the CPU.

### *Input and Output Primitives*

Microprocessors can provide programming support for input and output in two ways: I/O instructions and memory-mapped I/O. Some architectures, such as the Intel x86, provide special instructions (in and out in the case of the Intel x86) for input and output. These instructions provide a separate address space for I/O devices. But the most common way to implement I/O is by memory mapping—even CPUs that provide I/O instructions can also implement memory-mapped I/O. As the name implies, memory-mapped I/O provides addresses for the registers in each I/O device. Programs use the CPU's normal read and write instructions to communicate with the devices. Example 3.1 illustrates memory-mapped I/O on the ARM.

### *Example 3.1*

### *Memory-mapped I/O on ARM*

We can use the EQU pseudo-op to define a symbolic name for the memory location of our I/O device:

DEV1 EQU 0x1000

Given that name, we can use the following standard code to read and write the device register:

LDR r1,#DEV1 ; set up device address

LDR r0,[r1] ; read DEV1

LDR r0,#8; set up value to write

STR r0,[r1] ; write 8 to device

How can we directly write I/O devices in a high-level language like C? When we define and use a variable in C, the compiler hides the variable's address from us. But we can use pointers to manipulate addresses of I/O devices.

The traditional names for functions that read and write arbitrary memory locations are peek and poke.

The peek function can be written in C as:

intpeek(char *location) {

return *location; /* de-reference

location pointer */

}

The argument to peek is a pointer that is de- referenced by the C * operator to read the location.

Thus, to read a device register we can write:

#define DEV1 0x1000

...

dev_status = peek(DEV1); /* read device

register */

The poke function can be implemented as:

void poke(char *location,  char  newval) {

(*location) = newval; /* write to

location */

}

To write to the status register, we can use the following code:

poke(DEV1,8); /* write 8 to device

register */

These functions can, of course, be used to read and write   arbitrary memory locations, not just devices.

## Busy-Wait I/O

The most basic way to use devices in a program is busy-wait I/O . Devices are typically slower than the CPU and may require many cycles to complete an operation.

If the CPU is performing multiple operations on a single device, such as writing several characters to an output device, then it must wait for one operation to complete before starting the next one.

(If we try to start writing the second character before the device has finished with the first one, for example, the device will probably never print the first character.) Asking an I/O device whether it is finished by reading its status register is often called polling .

Example 3.2 illustrates busy-wait I/O.

## Example 3.2

### Busy-wait I/O programming

In this example we want to write a sequence of characters to an output device. The device has two registers: one for the character to be written and a status register. The status register's value is 1 when the device is busy writing and 0 when the write transaction has completed.

We will use the peek and poke functions to write the busy-wait routine in C. First, we define symbolic names for the register addresses:

```c
#define OUT_CHAR 0x1000 /* output device character

register */

#define OUT_STATUS 0x1001 /* output device status

register */
```

The sequence of characters is stored in a standard C string, which is terminated by a null (0) character. We can use peek and poke to send the characters and wait for each transaction to complete:

```c
char *mystring = "Hello, world." /* string to write */

char *current_char; /* pointer to current position in

string*/

current_char = mystring; /* point to head of string */

while (*current_char != '\ 0') { /* until null character

*/

poke(OUT_CHAR,*current_char); /* send character to

device */

while (peek(OUT_STATUS) != 0); /* keep checking status

*/

current_char++; /* update character pointer */

}
```

Example 3.3 illustrates a combination of input and output.

*Example 3.3*

***Copying Characters from Input to Output using Busy-Wait I/O***

We want to repeatedly read a character from the input device and write it to the output device. First, we need to define the addresses for the device registers:

#define IN_DATA 0x1000

#define IN_STATUS 0x1001

#define OUT_DATA 0x1100

#define OUT_STATUS 0x1101

The input device sets its status register to 1 when a new character has been read; we must set the status register back to 0 after the character has been read so that the device is ready to read another character. When writing, we must set the output status register to 1 to start writing and wait for it to return to 0. We can use peek and poke to repeatedly perform the read/write operation:

```
while (TRUE)        { /* perform operation forever */
/* read a character into achar */
while (peek(IN_STATUS) == 0); /* wait until ready
*/
achar = (char)peek(IN_DATA); /* read the character
*/
/* write achar */ poke(OUT_DATA,achar);
poke(OUT_STATUS,1); /* turn on device */
while (peek(OUT_STATUS) != 0); /* wait until done */
}
```

### Interrupts

### Basics

Busy-wait I/O is extremely inefficient-the CPU does nothing but test the device status while the I/O transaction is in progress.

In many cases, the CPU could do useful work in parallel with the I/O transaction, such as:

1. computation, as in determining the next output to send to the device or processing the last input received, and
2. control of other I/O devices.

To allow parallelism, we need to introduce new mechanisms into the CPU.

The interrupt mechanism allows devices to signal the CPU and to force execution of a particular piece of code. When an interrupt occurs, the program counter's value is changed to point to an interrupt handler routine (also commonly known as a device driver) that takes care of the device: writing the next data, reading data that have just become ready, and so on.

The interrupt mechanism of course saves the value of the PC at the interruption so that the CPU can return to the program that was interrupted. Interrupts therefore allow the flow of control in the CPU to change easily between different contexts, such as a foreground computation and multiple I/O devices.

As shown in Figure 3.2, the interface between the CPU and I/O device includes the following signals for interrupting:

- The I/O device asserts the interrupt request signal when it wants service from the CPU; and
- The CPU asserts the interrupt acknowledge signal when it is ready to handle the I/O device's request.

The I/O device's logic decides when to interrupt; for example, it may generate an interrupt when its status register goes into the ready state.

The CPU may not be able to immediately service an interrupt request because it may be doing something else that must be finished first—for example, a program that talks to both a high-speed disk drive and a low-speed keyboard should be designed to finish a disk transaction before handling a keyboard interrupt. Only when the CPU decides to acknowledge the interrupt does the CPU change the program counter to point to the device's handler.

The interrupt handler operates much like a subroutine, except that it is not called by the executing program.

The program that runs when no interrupt is being handled is often called the foreground program; when the interrupt handler finishes, it returns to the foreground program, wherever processing was interrupted

***Example 3.5***

***Copying Characters from Input to Output with Interrupts and Buffers***

Because we do not need to wait for each character, we can make this I/O program more sophisticated than the one in Example 3.4. Rather than reading a single character and then writing it, the program performs reads and writes independently. The read and write routines communicate through the following global variables:

1) A character string io_buf will hold a queue of characters that have been read but not yetwritten.

   - A pair of integers buf_start and buf_end will point to the first and last characters read.

   - A integer error will be set to 0 whenever io_buf overflows.

   - The global variables allow the input and output devices to run at different rates. The queue io_buf acts as a wraparound buffer—we add characters to the tail when an input is received and take characters from the tail when we are ready for output. The head and tail wrap around the end of the buffer array to make most efficient use of the array. Here is the situation at the start of the program's execution, where the tail points to the first available character and the head points to the ready character. As seen below, because the head and tail are equal, we know that the queue

When the first character is read, the tail is incremented after the character is added to the queue, leaving the buffer and pointers looking like the following:

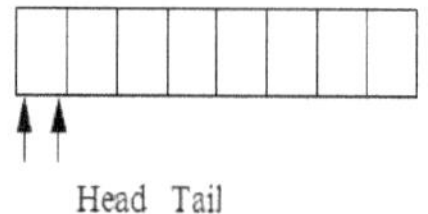



When the buffer is full, we leave one character in the buffer unused. As the next figure shows, if we added another character and updated the tail buffer (wrapping it around to the head of the buffer), we would be unable to distinguish a full buffer from an empty one.

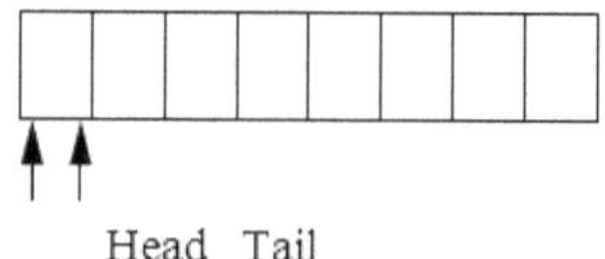

Here is what happens when the output goes past the end of io_buf:

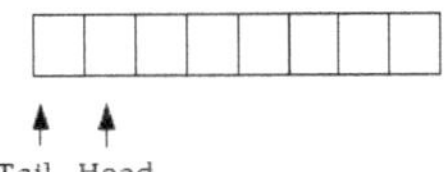



The following code provides the declarations for the above global variables and some service routines for adding and removing characters from the queue. Because interrupt handlers are regular code, we can use subroutines to structure code just as with any program.

```c
#define BUF_SIZE 8
char io_buf[BUF_SIZE]; /* character buffer */
int buf_head = 0, buf_tail = 0; /* current position
in buffer */
int error = 0; /* set to 1 if buffer ever  overflows
*/
void empty_buffer() { /* returns TRUE if buffer is
empty */
buf_head  == buf_tail;
}
void full_buffer()
{
/* returns TRUE if  buffer is full */ (buf_tail+1) % BUF_SIZE  == buf_head ;
}
int nchars()
{ /* returns the number of characters
in  the buffer */
if (buf_head >= buf_tail) return buf_tail -
buf_head;
else  return BUF_SIZE  + buf_tail - buf_head;
}
void add_char(char achar)
{ /* add a character to
the  buffer head */
io_buf[buf_tail++]   = achar;
/* check pointer */
if (buf_tail == BUF_SIZE)
```

```c
    buf_tail = 0;
}
char remove_char() { /* take a character from the
buffer head */
char achar;
achar  =  io_buf[buf_head++];
/* check pointer */
if (buf_head == BUF_SIZE) buf_head  = 0;
}
```

Assume that we have two interrupt handling routines defined in C, input_handler for the input device and output_handler for the output device. These routines work with the device in much the same way as did the busy-wait routines. The only complication is in starting the output device: If io_buf has characters waiting, the output driver can start a new output transaction by itself. But if there are no characters waiting, an outside agent must start a new output action whenever the new character arrives. Rather than force the foreground program to look at the character buffer, we will have the input handler check to see whether there is only one character in the buffer and start a new transaction.

Here is the code for the input handler:

```c
#define IN_DATA 0x1000
#define IN_STATUS 0x1001 void  input_handler() { char  achar;
if  (full_buffer()) /* error */
error  = 1;
else {
/* read the  character and update pointer */ achar = peek(IN_DATA);
/* read character */ add_char(achar);
/* add to  queue */
}
poke(IN_STATUS,0); /* set status  register back to  0
*/
/* if  buffer was empty, start a new output transaction
*/
if  (nchars() == 1) { /* buffer had been empty until this
interrupt */
poke(OUT_DATA,remove_char()); /* send character */
```

```
poke(OUT_STATUS,1); /* turn device on */
}
#define  OUT_DATA 0x1100
#define OUT_STATUS 0x1101 void output_handler()
{ if (!empty_buffer())  { /* start        a new character */
poke(OUT_DATA,remove_char()); /* send character */
poke(OUT_STATUS,1); /* turn device on */
}
}
```

The foreground program does not need to do anything—everything is taken care of by the interrupt handlers. The foreground program is free to do useful work as it is occasionally interrupted by input and output operations. The following sample execution of the program in the form of a UML sequence diagram shows how input and output are interleaved with the foreground program. (We have kept the last input character in the queue until output is complete to make it clearer when input occurs.) The simulation shows that the foreground program is not executing continuously, but it continues to run in its regular state independent of the number of characters waiting in the queue.

Interrupts allow a lot of concurrency, which can make very efficient use of the CPU. But when the interrupt handlers are buggy, the errors can be very hard to find. The fact that an interrupt can occur at any time means that the same bug can manifest itself in different ways when the interrupt handler interrupts different segments of the foreground program. Example 3.6 illustrates the problems inherent in debugging interrupt handlers.

### *Example 3.6*

### *Debugging Interrupt Code*

Assume that the foreground code is performing a matrix multiplication operation y Ax b:

```
for (i = 0; i < M; i++)

{

y[i] = b[i];

for (j = 0; j < N; j++)

y[i] = y[i] + A[i,j]*x[j];

}
```

What happens to the foreground program when j changes value during an interrupt depends on when the interrupt handler executes. Because the value of j is reset at each iteration of the outer loop, the bug will affect only one entry of the result y . But clearly the entry that changes will depend on when the interrupt occurs. Furthermore, the change observed in y depends on not only what new value is assigned to j (which may depend on the data handled by the interrupt code), but also when in the inner loop the interrupt occurs. An interrupt at the beginning of the inner loop will give a different result than one that occurs near the end. The number of possible new values for the result vector is much too large to consider manually—the bug cannot be found by enumerating the possible wrong values and correlating them with a given root cause. The CPU implements interrupts by checking the interrupt request line at the beginning of execution of every instruction. If an interrupt request has been asserted, the CPU does not fetch the instruction pointed to by the PC. Instead the CPU sets the PC to a predefined location, which is the beginning of the interrupt

### *Priorities and Vectors*

Providing a practical interrupt system requires having more than a simple interrupt request line. Most systems have more than one I/O device, so there must be some mechanism for allowing multiple devices to interrupt. We also want to have flexibility in the locations of the interrupt handling routines, the addresses for devices, and so on. There are two ways in which interrupts can be generalized to handle multiple devices and to provide more flexible definitions for the associated hardware and software:

1. Interrupt priorities allow the CPU to recognize some interrupts as more important than others, and

2. Interrupt vectors allow the interrupting device to specify its handler. Prioritized interrupts not only allow multiple devices to be connected to the interrupt line but also allow the CPU to ignore less important interrupt requests while it handles more important requests. As shown in Figure 3.3, the CPU pro- vides several different interrupt request signals, shown here as L1, L2, up to Ln. Typically, the lower-numbered interrupt lines are given higher priority, so in this case, if devices 1, 2, and n all requested

Interrupts simultaneously, 1's request would be acknowledged because it is connected to the highest-priority interrupt line. Rather than provide a separate interrupt acknowledge line for each device, most CPUs use a set of signals that provide the priority number of the winning interrupt in binary form (so that interrupt level 7 requires 3 bits rather than 7). A device knows that its interrupt request was accepted by seeing its own priority number on the interrupt acknowledge lines.

### Example 3.7

### I/O with Prioritized Interrupts

Assume that we have devices A, B, and C. A has priority 1 (highest priority), B priority 2, and C priority 3. The following UML sequence diagram shows which interrupt handler is executing as a function of time for a sequence of interrupt requests. In each case, an interrupt handler keeps running until either it is finished or a higher- priority interrupt arrives. The C interrupt, although it arrives early, does not finish for a  long time because  interrupts from both A and B intervene—system design must take into account the worst-case combinations of interrupts that can occur to ensure that no device goes without service for too long. When both A and B interrupt simultaneously, A's interrupt gets priority; when A's handler is finished, the priority mechanism automatically answers  B's pending interrupt

Vectors provide flexibility in a different dimension, namely, the ability to define the interrupt handler that should service a request from  a  device. Figure 3.5 shows the hardware structure required to support interrupt vectors. In addition to the interrupt request and acknowledge lines, additional interrupt vector lines run from the devices to the CPU. After a device's request is acknowledged, it sends its interrupt vector over those lines to the CPU. The CPU then uses the vector number as an index in a table stored in memory as shown in Figure 3.5. The location referenced in the interrupt vector table by the vector number gives the address  of the handler.

There are two important things to notice about the interrupt vector mechanism.  First, Most modern CPUs implement both prioritized and vectored interrupts. Priori- ties determine which device is serviced first, and vectors determine what routine is used to service the interrupt. The combination of the two provides a rich interface between hardware and software.

Interrupt overhead Now that we have a basic understanding of the interrupt mechanism, we can consider the complete interrupt handling process. Once a device requests an interrupt, some steps are performed by the CPU, some by the device, and others by software. Here are the major steps in the process:

1.  CPU The CPU checks for pending interrupts at the beginning of an instruction.  It answers the highest-priority interrupt, which has a higher  priority than that given in the interrupt priority register.

2. Device The device receives the acknowledgment and sends the CPU its interrupt vector.

3. CPU The CPU looks up the device handler address in the interrupt vector table using the vector as an index. A subroutine-like mechanism is used to save the current value of the PC and possibly other internal CPU state, such as general-purpose registers.

4. Software The device driver may save additional CPU state. It then performs the required.

  - **CPU** The interrupt return instruction restores the PC and other automatically saved states to return execution to the code that was interrupted.

  - Interrupts do not come without a performance penalty. In addition to the execution time required for the code that talks directly to the devices, there is execution time overhead associated with the interrupt mechanisms.

  - The **interrupt** itself has overhead similar to a subroutine call. Because an interrupt causes a change in the program counter, it incurs a branch penalty. In addition, if the interrupt automatically stores CPU registers, that action requires extra cycles, even if the state is not modified by the interrupt handler.

  - In addition to the **branch** delay penalty, the interrupt requires extra cycles to acknowledge the interrupt and obtain the vector from the device.

  - The interrupt **handler** will, in general, save and restore CPU registers that were not automatically saved by the interrupt.

  - The interrupt **return** instruction incurs a branch penalty as well as the time required to restore the automatically saved state.

The time required for the hardware to respond to the interrupt, obtain the vector, and so on cannot be changed by the programmer. In particular, CPUs vary quite a bit in the amount of internal state automatically saved by an interrupt. The programmer does have control over what state is modified by the interrupt handler and therefore it must be saved and restored. Careful programming can sometimes result in a small number of registers used by an interrupt handler, thereby saving time in maintaining the CPU state. However, such tricks usually require coding the interrupt handler in assembly language rather than a high-level language.

Interrupts in ARM ARM7 supports two types of interrupts: fast interrupt requests (FIQs) and interrupt requests (IRQs). An FIQ takes priority over an IRQ. The interrupt table is always kept in the bottom memory addresses, starting at location 0. The entries in the table typically contain subroutine calls to the appropriate handler.

The ARM7 performs the following steps when responding to an interrupt [ARM99B]:

- saves the appropriate value of the PC to be used to return,
- copies the CPSR into a saved program status register (SPSR),
- Forces bits in the CPSR to note the interrupt, an forces the PC to the appropriate interrupt vector. When leaving the interrupt handler, the handler should:
- restore the proper PC value,
- restore the CPSR from the SPSR, and
- clear interrupt disable flags.

The worst-case latency to respond to an interrupt includes the following components:

- two cycles to synchronize the external request,
- up to 20 cycles to complete the current instruction,
- three cycles for data abort, and
- two cycles to enter the interrupt handling state.

This adds up to 27 clock cycles. The best-case latency is four clock cycles. Interrupts in C55x Interrupts in the C55x [Tex04] never take less than seven clock cycles. In many situations, they take 13 clock cycles. A maskable interrupt is processed n severalsteps once the interrupt request is sent to the CPU:

- The interrupt flag register (IFR) corresponding to the interrupt is set.
- The interrupt enable register (IER) is checked to ensure that the interrupt is enabled.
- The interrupt mask register (INTM) is checked to be sure that the interrupt is not masked.
- The interrupt flag register (IFR) corresponding to the flag is cleared.
- Appropriate registers are saved as context.
- INTM is set to 1 to disable maskable interrupts.
- DGBM is set to 1 to disable debug events.
- EALLOW is set to 0 to disable access to non-CPU emulation registers.
- A branch is performed to the interrupt service routine (ISR).

The C55x provides two mechanisms—fast-return and slow-return— to save and restore registers for interrupts and other context switches. Both processes save the return address and loop context registers. The fast-return mode uses RETA to save the return address and CFCT for the loop context bits. The slow return mode, in contrast, saves the return address and loop context bits on the stack.

## Supervisor Mode, Exceptions, and Traps

### *Supervisor Mode*

As will become clearer in later chapters, complex systems are often implemented as several programs that communicate with each other. These programs may run under the command of an operating system.

It may be desirable to provide hardware checks to ensure that the programs do not interfere with each other-for example, by erroneously writing into a segment of memory used by another program. Soft- ware debugging is important but can leave some problems in a running system; hardware checks ensure an additional level of safety.

In such cases it is often useful to have a supervisor mode provided by the CPU. Normal programs run in user mode. The supervisor mode has privileges that user modes do not. For example, we study memory management systems in Section 3.4.2 that allow the addresses of memory locations to be changed dynamically.

Control of the memory management unit (MMU) is typically reserved for supervisor mode to avoid the obvious problems that could occur when program bugs cause inadvertent changes in the memory management registers.

Not all CPUs have supervisor modes. Many DSPs, including the C55x, do not provide supervisor modes. The ARM, however, does have such a mode.

The ARM instruction that puts the CPU in supervisor mode is called SWI:

SWI CODE_1

It can, of course, be executed conditionally, as with any ARM instruction. SWI causes the CPU to go into supervisor mode and sets the PC to 0x08. The argument to SWI is a 24-bit immediate value that is passed on to the supervisor mode code; it allows the program to request various services from the supervisor mode.

In supervisor mode, the bottom 5 bits of the CPSR are all set to 1 to indicate that the CPU is in supervisor mode.

The old value of the CPSR just before the SWI is stored in a register called the saved program status register (SPSR). There are in fact several SPSRs for different modes; the supervisor mode SPSR is referred to as SPSR_svc.

To return from supervisor mode, the supervisor restores the PC from register r14 and restores the CPSR from the SPSR_svc.

### *Exceptions*

An exception is an internally detected error. A simple example is division by zero. One way to handle this problem would be to check every divisor before division to be sure it is not zero, but this would both substantially increase the size of numerical programs and cost a great deal of CPU time evaluating the divisor's value. The CPU can more efficiently check the divisor's value during execution. Since the time at which a zero divisor will be found is not known in advance, this event is similar to an interrupt except that it is generated inside the CPU. The exception mechanism provides a way for the program to react to such unexpected events.

### *Traps*

A trap, also known as a software interrupt, is an instruction that explicitly generates an exception condition. The most common use of a trap is to enter supervisor mode. The entry into supervisor mode must be controlled to maintain security—if the interface between user and supervisor mode is improperly designed, a user pro- gram may be able to sneak code into the supervisor mode that could be executed to perform harmful operations.

The ARM provides the SWI interrupt for software interrupts. This instruction causes the CPU to enter supervisor mode. An opcode is embedded in the instruction that can be read by the handler.

## Co-Processors

CPU architects often want to provide flexibility in what features are implemented in the CPU. One way to provide such flexibility at the instruction set level is to allow co-processors, which are attached to the CPU and implement some of the instructions. For example, floating-point arithmetic was introduced into the Intel architecture by providing separate chips that implemented the floating-point instructions.

To support co-processors, certain opcodes must be reserved in the instruction set for coprocessor operations. Because it executes instructions, a co-processor must be tightly coupled to the CPU. When the CPU receives a co-processor instruction, the CPU must activate the co- processor and pass it the relevant instruction. Co-processor instructions can load and store co-processor registers or can perform internal operations. The CPU can suspend execution to wait for the co-processor instruction to finish; it can also take a more superscalar approach and continue executing instructions while waiting for the coprocessor to finish.

## Memory System Mechanisms

Modern microprocessors do more than just read and write a monolithic memory. Architectural features improve both the speed and capacity of memory systems.

Microprocessor clock rates are increasing at a faster rate than memory speeds, such that memories are falling further and further behind microprocessors every day. As a result, computer architects resort to caches to increase the average performance of the memory system. Although memory capacity is increasing steadily, program sizes are increasing as well, and designers may not be willing to pay for all the memory demanded by an application. Modern microprocessor units (MMUs) perform address translations that provide a larger virtual memory space in a small physical memory. In this section, we review both caches and MMUs.

### *Caches*

Caches are widely used to speed up memory system performance. Many microprocessor architectures include caches as part of their definition. The cache speeds up average memory access time when properly used. It increases the variability of memory access times—accesses in the cache will be fast, while access to locations not cached will be slow. This variability in performance makes it especially important to understand how caches work so that we can better understand how to predict cache performance and factor variabilities into system design.

A cache is a small, fast memory that holds copies of some of the contents of main memory. Because the cache is fast, it provides higher-speed access for the CPU; but since it is small, not all requests can be satisfied by the cache, forcing the system to wait for the slower main memory. Caching makes sense when the CPU is using only a relatively small set of memory locations at any one time; the set of active locations is often called the working set.

Shows how the cache support reads in the memory system. A cache controller mediates between the CPU and the memory system comprised of the main memory. The cache controller sends a memory request to the cache and main memory.

If the requested location is in the cache, the cache controller forwards the location's contents to the CPU and aborts the main memory request; this condition is known as a cache hit. If the location is not in the cache, the controller waits for the value from main memory and forwards it to the CPU; this situation is known as a cache miss.

We can classify cache misses into several types depending on the situation that generated them:

- a compulsory miss (also known as a cold miss) occurs the first time a location is used,
- a capacity miss is caused by a too-large working set, and
- a conflict miss happens when two locations map to the same location in the cache.

Even before we consider ways to implement caches, we can write some basic formulas for memory system performance. Let h be the hit rate, the probability that a given memory location is in the cache. It follows that 1 h is the miss rate, or the probability that the location is not in the cache. Then we can compute the average memory access time as

$$t_{av} \quad h t_{cache} \quad (1 \quad h) t_{main}. \quad (3.1)$$

where tcache is the access time of the cache and tmain is the main memory access time. The memory access times are basic parameters available from the memory manufacturer. The hit rate depends on the program being executed and the cache organization, and is typically measured using simulators, as is described in more detail in Section 5.6. The best-case memory access time (ignoring cache controller overhead) is tcache, while the worst-case access time is tmain. Given that tmain is typically 50–60 ns for DRAM, while tcache is at most a few nanoseconds, the spread between worst-case and best-case memory delays is substantial.

Modern CPUs may use multiple levels of cache as shown in Figure

3.7. The first-level cache (commonly known as L1 cache) is closest to the CPU, the second-level cache (L2 cache) feeds the first-level cache, and so on. The second-level cache is much larger but is also slower. If h1 is the first-level hit rate and h2 is the rate at which access hit the second-level cache but not the first-level cache, then the average access time for a two-level cache system is tav h1 tL1 h2 tL2 (1 h1 h2 )tmain

The simplest way to implement a cache is a direct-mapped cache, as shown in Figure 3.8. The cache consists of cache blocks, each of which includes a tag to show which memory location is represented by this block, a data field holding the contents of that memory, and a valid tag to show whether the contents of this cache block are valid. An address is divided into three sections. The index is used to select which cache block to check. The tag is compared against the tag value in the block selected by the index. If the address tag matches the tag value in the block, that block includes the desired memory location. If the length of the data field is longer than the minimum addressable unit, then the lowest bits of the address are used as an offset to select the required value from the data field. Given the structure of the cache, there is only one block that must be checked to see whether a location is in the cache—the index uniquely determines that block. If the access is a hit, the data value is read from the cache.

Writes are slightly more complicated than reads because we have to update main memory as well as the cache. There are several methods by which we can do this. The simplest scheme is known as write-through— every write changes both the cache and the corresponding main memory location (usually through a write buffer). This scheme ensures that the cache and main memory are consistent, but may generate some additional main memory traffic. We can reduce the number of times we write to main memory by using a write-back policy:If we write only when we remove a location from the cache, we eliminate the writes when a location is written several times before it is removed from the cache.

The direct-mapped cache is both fast and relatively low cost, but it does have limits in its caching power due to its simple scheme for mapping the cache onto main memory. Consider a direct-mapped cache with four blocks, in which locations 0, 1, 2, and 3 all map to different blocks. But locations 4, 8, 12, ... all map to the same block as location 0; locations 1, 5, 9, 13, ... all map to a single block; and so on. If two popular locations in a program happen to map onto the same block, we will not gain the full benefits of the cache. As seen in Section 5.6, this can create program performance problems.

The limitations of the direct-mapped cache can be reduced by going to the set-associative cache structure shown in Figure 3.9. A set-associative cache is characterized by the number of banks or ways it uses, giving an n-way set- associative cache. A set is formed by all the blocks (one for each bank) that share the same index. Each set is implemented with a direct-mapped cache. A cache request is broadcast to all banks simultaneously. If any of the sets has the location, the cache reports a hit. Although memory locations map onto blocks using the same function, there are n separate blocks for each set of locations. Therefore, we can simultaneously cache several locations that happen to map onto the same cache block. The set-associative cache structure incurs a little extra overhead and is slightly slower than a direct-mapped cache, but the higher hit rates that it can provide often compensate.

The set-associative cache generally provides higher hit rates than the direct- mapped cache because conflicts between a small number of locations can be resolved within the cache. The set-associative cache is somewhat slower, so the CPU designer has to be careful that it doesn't slow down the CPU's cycle time too much. A more important problem with set-associative caches for embedded program Various ARM implementations use different cache sizes and organizations [Fur96]. The ARM600 includes a 4-KB, 64-way (wow!) unified instruction/data cache. The StrongARM uses a 16-KB, 32-way instruction cache with a 32-byte block and a 16-KB,32-way data cache with a 32-byte block;the data cache uses a write-back strategy.

The C5510, one of the models of C55x, uses a 16-K byte instruction cache organized as a two-way set-associative cache with four 32-bit words per line. The instruction cache can be disabled by software if desired. It also includes two RAM sets that are designed to hold large contiguous blocks of code. Each RAM set can hold up to 4-K bytes of code organized as 256 lines of four 32-bit words per line. Each RAM has a tag that specifies what range of addresses are in the RAM; it also includes a tag valid field to show whether the RAM is in use and line valid bits for each line.

### *Memory Management Units and Address Translation*

A MMU translates addresses between the CPU and physical memory. This translation process is often known as memory mapping since addresses are mapped from a logical space into a physical space. MMUs in embedded systems appear primarily in the host processor. It is helpful to understand the basics of MMUs for embedded systems complex enough to require them.

Many DSPs, including the C55x, do not use MMUs. Since DSPs are used for compute-intensive tasks, they often do not require the hardware assist for logical address spaces.

Early computers used MMUs to compensate for limited address space in their instruction sets. When memory became cheap enough that physical memory could be larger than the address space defined by instructions, MMUs allowed software to manage multiple programs in a single physical memory, each with its own address space. Because modern CPUs typically do not have this limitation, MMUs are used to provide virtual addressing.

As shown in Figure 3.10, the MMU accepts logical addresses from the CPU. Logical addresses refer to the program's abstract address space but do not correspond to actual RAM locations.

The MMU translates them from tables to physical addresses that do correspond to RAM. By changing the MMU's tables, you can change the physical location at which the program resides without modifying the program's code or data. (We must, of course, move the program in main memory to correspond to the memory mapping change.)

Furthermore, if we add a secondary storage unit such as flash or a disk, we can eliminate parts of the program from main memory.

In a virtual memory system, the MMU keeps track of which logical addresses are actually resident in main memory; those that do not reside in main memory are kept on the secondary storage device. When the CPU requests an address that is not in main memory, the MMU generates an exception called a page fault.

The handler for this exception executes code that reads the requested location from the secondary storage device into main memory. The program that generated the page fault is restarted by the handler only after

- the required memory has been read back into main memory, and
- the MMU's tables have been updated to reflect the changes.

Of course, loading a location into main memory will usually require throwing something out of main memory. The displaced memory is copied into secondary storage before the requested location is read in. As with caches, LRU is a good replacement policy.

There are two styles of address translation: segmented and paged . Each has advantages and the two can be combined to form a segmented, paged addressing scheme. As illustrated in Figure 3.11, segmenting is designed to support a large, arbitrarily sized region of memory, while pages describe small, equally sized regions.

A segment is usually described by its start address and size, allowing different segments to be of different sizes. Pages are of uniform size, which simplifies the hardware required for address translation. A segmented, paged scheme is created by dividing each segment into pages and using two steps for address translation. Paging introduces the possibility of fragmentation as program pages are scattered around physical memory.

In a simple segmenting scheme, shown in Figure 3.12, the MMU would maintain a segment register that describes the currently active segment. This register would point to the base of the current segment. The address extracted from an instruction (or from any other source for addresses, such as a register) would be used as the offset for the address. The physical address is formed by adding the segment base to the offset. Most segmentation schemes also check the physical address against the upper limit of the segment by extending the segment register to include the segment size and comparing the offset to the allowed size. The translation of paged addresses requires more MMU state but a simpler calculation. As shown in Figure 3.13, the logical address is divided into two sections, including a page number and an offset. The page number is used as an index into a page table, which stores the physical address for the start of each page. However, Segments and pages.

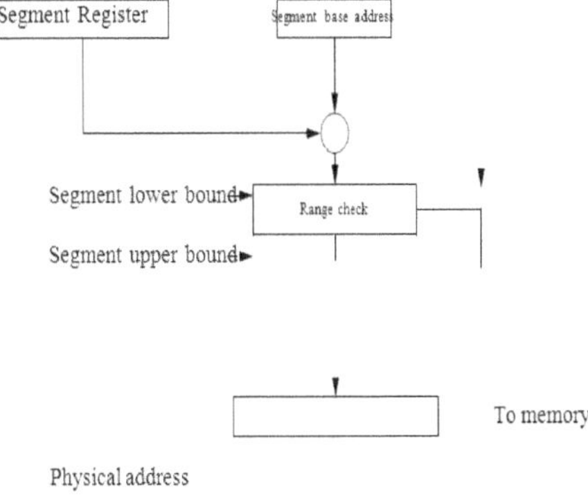



Figure 3.12: Address Translation for a Segment

Alternative schemes for organizing page tables.

- A dirty bit shows whether the page/segment has been written to. This bit is maintained by the MMU, since it knows about every write performed by the CPU.
- Permission bits are often used. Some pages/segments may be readable but not writable. If the CPU supports modes, pages/segments may be accessible by the supervisor but not in user mode.

A data or instruction cache may operate either on logical or physical addresses, depending on where it is positioned relative to the MMU. A MMU is an optional part of the ARM architecture. The ARM MMU supports both virtual address translation and memory protection; the architecture requires that the MMU be implemented when cache or write buffers are implemented. The ARM MMU supports the following types of memory regions for address translation:

- a section is a 1-MB block of memory,
- a large page is 64 KB, and
- a small page is 4 KB.

An address is marked as section mapped or page mapped. A two-level scheme is used to translate addresses. The first-level table, which is pointed to by the translation table Base register, holds descriptors for section translation and pointers to the second-level tables. The second-level tables describe the translation of both large and small pages. The basic two-level process for a large or small page is illustrated in Figure 3.15. The details differ between large and small pages, such as the size of the second-level table index. The first and second-level pages also contain access control bits for virtual memory and protection.

## CPU Performance

Now that we have an understanding of the various types of instructions that CPUs can execute, we can move on to a topic particularly important in embedded computing: How fast can the CPU execute instructions? In this section, we consider three factors that can substantially influence program performance: pipelining and caching.

### *Pipelining*

Modern CPUs are designed as pipelined machines in which several instructions are executed in parallel. Pipelining greatly increases the efficiency of the CPU. But like any pipeline, a CPU pipeline works best when its contents flow smoothly. Some sequences of instructions can disrupt the flow of information in the pipeline and, temporarily at least, slow down the operation of the CPU. The ARM7 has a three-stage pipeline:

- Fetch the instruction is fetched from memory.j
- Decode the instruction's opcode and operands are decoded to determine what function to perform.
- Execute the decoded instruction is executed.

Each of these operations requires one clock cycle for typical instructions. Thus, a normal instruction requires three clock cycles to completely execute, known as the latency of instruction execution. But since the pipeline has three stages, an instruction is completed in every clock cycle. In other words, the pipeline has a throughput of one instruction per cycle. Figure 3.16 illustrates the position of instructions in the pipeline during execution using the notation introduced by Hennessy and Patterson [Hen06]. A vertical slice through the timeline shows all instructions in the pipeline at that time. By following an instruction horizontally, we can see the progress of its execution. The C55x includes a seven-stage pipeline[Tex00B]:

- Fetch.
- Decode.
- Address computes data and branch addresses.
- Access 1 reads data.
- Access 2 finishes data read.
- Read stage puts operands onto internal busses.
- Execute performs operations.

RISC machines are designed to keep the pipeline busy. CISC machines may display a wide variation in instruction timing. Pipelined RISC machines typically have more regular timing characteristics—most instructions that do not have pipeline hazards display the same latency.

add r0,r1,#5 sub  r2,r3,r6

cmp r2,#3

The one-cycle-per-instruction completion rate does not hold in every case, however. The simplest case for extended execution is when an instruction is too complex to complete the execution phase in a single cycle. A multiple load instruction is an example of an instruction that requires several cycles in the execution phase. Figure 3.17 illustrates a data stall in the execution of a sequence of instructions starting with a load multiple (LDMIA) instruction. Since there are two registers to load, the instruction must stay in the execution phase for two cycles. In a multiphase execution, the decode stage is also occupied, since it must continue to remember the decoded instruction. As a result, the SUB instruction is fetched at the normal time but not decoded until the LDMIA is finishing. This delays the fetching of the third instruction, the CMP.

Branches also introduce control stall delays into the pipeline, commonly referred to as the branch penalty, as shown in Figure 3.18. The decision whether to take the conditional branch BNE is not made until the third clock cycle of that instruction's execution, which computes the branch target address. If the branch is taken, the succeeding instruction at PC+4 has been fetched and started to be decoded. When the branch is taken, the branch target address is used to fetch the branch target instruction. Since we have to wait for the execution cycle to complete before knowing the target, we must throw away two cycles of work on instructions in the path not taken. The CPU uses the two cycles between starting to fetch the branch target and starting to execute that instruction to finish housekeeping tasks related to the execution of the branch.

One way around this problem is to introduce the delayed branch. In this style of branch instruction, some number of instructions directly after the branch are always executed, whether or not the branch is taken.

This allows the CPU to keep the pipeline full during execution of the branch. However, some of those instructions after the delayed branch may be no-ops. Any instruction in the delayed branch window must be valid for both execution paths, whether or not the branch is taken. If there are not enough instructions to fill the delayed branch window, it must be filled with no-ops.

Let's use this knowledge of instruction execution time to evaluate the execution time of some C code, as shown in Example 3.9.

*Example 3.9*

*Execution Time of a for Loop on the ARM*

We will use the C code for the FIR filter of Application Example 2.1:

for (i = 0, f = 0; i < N; i++)

f = f + c[i] * x[i]; We repeat the ARM code for this loop:

; loop initiation  code

MOV r0,#0  ; use r0 for i, set to 0

MOV r8,#0    ; use a  separate  index for  arrays

ADR r2,N      ; get  address for  N

LDR r1,[r2] ; get value of N for loop termination test

MOV r2,#0    ; use r2 for f, set  to  0

ADR r3,c      ;  load r3 with address of base of  c array

ADR r5,x      ; load r5 with address of base of x   array

; loop body

loop LDR r4,[r3,r8]    ; get  value  of  c[i] LDR r6,[r5,r8]

 get value of x[i] MUL r4,r4,r6 ; compute c[i]*x[i]

ADD r2,r2,r4 ; add into  running sum f

; update loop counter and array index

ADD r8,r8,#4; add  one  word offset  to array index

ADD r0,r0,#1 ; add 1 to i

; test for exit CMP r0,r1

BLT  loop      ; if  i < N, continue  loop

loopend...

Inspection of the code shows that the only instruction that may take more than  one cycle is the conditional branch in the loop test. We can count the number of instructions and associated  number  of clock cycles in each  block as  follows:

Block              Variable    # Instructions    # Cycles

The unconditional branch at the end of the  update  block always incurs  a branch  penalty of  two cycles. The BLT instruction in the test block incurs  a pipeline  delay of two cycles  when the branch is taken. That happens for all but the last iteration, when the instruction has an execution  time of t test,worst ; the  last  iteration  executes  in time t test,best . We can  write  a

formula for the total execution  time of the loop in cycles as

$$t_{loop} = t_{init} + N(t_{body} + t_{update}) + (N - 1)t_{test,worst} + t_{test,best}.$$

## *Caching*

The extra time required to access a memory location not in the cache is often called the cache miss penalty. The amount of variation depends on several factors in the system architecture, but a cache miss is often several clock cycles slower than a cache hit. The time required to access a memory  location depends on whether the requested location is in the cache. However, as we have seen, a location may not be in the cache for several reasons.

- At a compulsory miss, the location has not been referenced before.
- At a conflict miss, two particular memory locations are fighting for the same cache line.
- At a capacity miss, the program's working set is simply too large for the cache.

The contents of the cache can change considerably over the course of execution of a program. When we have several programs running concurrently on the CPU

## CPU Power Consumption

Power consumption is, in some situations, as important as execution time. In this section we study the characteristics of CPUs that influence power consumption and mechanisms provided by CPUs to control how much power they consume.

First, it is important to distinguish between energy and power. Power is, of course, energy consumption per unit time. Heat generation depends on power consumption. Battery life, on the other hand, most directly depends on energy consumption. Generally, we will use the term power as shorthand for energy and power consumption, distinguishing between them only when necessary. The high-level power consumption characteristics of CPUs and other system components are derived from the circuits used to build those components. Today, virtually all digital systems are built with complementary metal oxide semi- conductor (CMOS) circuitry. The detailed circuit characteristics are best  left  to a study  of VLSI design [Wol08], but the basic sources of CMOS power consumption are easily identified and  briefly described below.

- Voltage drops: The dynamic power consumption of a CMOS circuit is proportional to the square of the power supply voltage ($V^2$ ). Therefore, by reducing the power supply voltage to the lowest level that provides the required performance, we can significantly reduce power consumption. We also may be able to add parallel hardware and even further reduce the power supply voltage while maintaining required performance [Cha92].

- Toggling : A CMOS circuit uses most of its power when it is changing its output value. This provides two ways to reduce power consumption. By reducing the speed at which the circuit operates, we can reduce its power consumption (although not the total energy required for the operation, since the result is available later). We can actually reduce energy consumption by eliminating unnecessary changes to the inputs of a CMOS circuit-eliminating unnecessary glitches at the circuit outputs eliminates unnecessary power consumption.

- Leakage: Even when a CMOS circuit is not active, some charge leaks out of the circuit's nodes through the substrate. The only way to eliminate leak- age current is to remove the power supply. Completely disconnecting the power supply eliminates power consumption, but it usually takes a significant amount of time to reconnect the system to the power supply and reinitialize its internal state so that it once again performs properly

There are two types of power management features provided by CPUs. A static power management mechanism is invoked by the user but does not otherwise depend on CPU activities. An example of a static mechanism is a power- down mode intended to save energy. This mode provides a high-level way to reduce unnecessary power consumption. The mode is typically entered with an instruction. If the mode stops the interpretation of instructions, then it clearly cannot be exited by execution of another instruction. Power-down modes typically end upon receipt of an interrupt or other event. A dynamic power management mechanism takes actions to control power based upon the dynamic activity in the CPU. For example, the CPU may turn off certain sections of the CPU when the instructions being executed do not need them.

### Application Example 3.2

### Energy Efficiency Features in the PowerPC 603

The PowerPC 603 [Gar94] was designed specifically for low-power operation while retaining high performance. It typically dissipates 2.2 W running at 80 MHz. The architecture pro- vides three low-power modes—doze, nap, and sleep—that provide static power management capabilities for use by the programs and operating system.

The 603 also uses a variety of dynamic power management techniques for power minimization that are performed automatically, without program intervention. The CPU is a two-issue, out-of-order superscalar processor. It uses the dynamic techniques summarized below to reduce power consumption.

- An execution unit that is not being used can be shut down.
- The cache, an 8-KB, two-way set-associative cache, was organized into subarrays so that at most two out of eight subarrays will be accessed on any given clock cycle. A variety of circuit techniques were also used in the cache to reduce power consumption.

Not all units in the CPU are active all the time; idling them when they are not being used can save power. The table below shows the percentage of time various units in the 603 were idle for the SPEC integer and floating-point benchmarks [Gar94].

A system power manager can both monitor the CPU and other devices and control their operation to gracefully transition between power modes. It provides several registers that allow programs to control power modes, determine why power modes were entered, determine the current state of power management modes, and so on.

The SA-1100 provides the three power modes described below.

- Run mode is normal operation and has the highest power consumption.
- Idle mode saves power by stopping the CPU clock. The system unit modules-real- time clock, operating system timer, interrupt control, general-purpose I/O, and power manager-all remain operational. Idle mode is entered by executing a three-instruction sequence. The CPU returns to run mode upon receiving an interrupt from one of the internal system units or from a peripheral or by resetting the CPU. This causes the machine to restart the CPU clock and to resume execution where it left off.
- Sleep mode shuts off most of the chip's activity. Entering sleep mode causes the system to shut down on-chip activity, reset the CPU, and negate the PWR_EN pin to tell the external electronics that the chip's power supply should be driven to 0 V. A separate I/O power supply remains on and supplies power to the power manager so that the CPU can be awakened from sleep mode; the low-speed clock keeps the power manager running at low speeds sufficient to manage sleep mode. The CPU software should set several registers to prepare for sleep mode. Sleep mode is entered by forcing the sleep bit in the power manager control register; it can also be entered by a power supply fault. The sleep shutdown sequence happens in three steps, each of which requires about 30 s. The machine wakes up from sleep state on a preprogrammed wake-up

event. The wake-up sequence has three steps: the PWR_EN pin is asserted to turn on the external power supply and waits for about 10  ms; the 3.686-MHz oscillator is ramped up to speed; and the internal reset is negated and the CPU boot sequence begins.

Here is the power state machine of the SA-1100 [Ben00]:

$$P_{run}5400 \text{ mW}$$

The sleep mode saves over three orders of magnitude of power consumption. However, the time required to reenter run mode from sleep is over a tenth of a second.

The SA-1100 has a companion chip, the SA-1111, that provides an integrated set of peripherals. That chip has its own power management modes that complement the SA-1100.

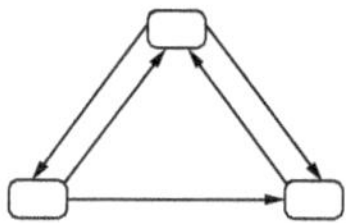

## Data Compressor

Our design example for this chapter is a data compressor that takes in data with a constant number of bits per data element and puts out a compressed data stream in which the data is encoded in variable-length symbols. Because this chapter concentrates on CPUs, we focus on the data compression routine itself.

### *Requirements and Algorithm*

We use the Huffman coding technique, which is introduced in Application Example 3.4. We require some understanding of how our compression code fits into a larger system. Figure 3.20 shows a collaboration diagram for the data compression process. The data compressor takes in a sequence of input symbols and then produces a stream of output symbols. Assume for simplicity that the input symbols are one byte in length.The output symbols are variable length,so we have to choose a format in which to deliver the output data. Delivering each coded symbol separately is tedious, since we would have to supply the length of each symbol and use external code to pack them into words. On the other hand, bit-by-bit delivery is almost certainly too slow. Therefore, we will rely on the data compressor to pack the coded symbols into an array. There is not a one-to-one relationship between the input and output symbols, and we may have to wait for several input symbols before a packed output word comes out.

*Application Example 3.4*

## Huffman Coding for Text Compression

Text compression algorithms aim at statistical reductions in the volume of data. One commonly used compression algorithm is Huffman coding [Huf52], which makes use of information.

The data compressor as discussed above is not a complete system, but we can create at least a partial requirements list for the module as seen below. We used the abbreviation N/A for not applicable to describe some items that do not make sense for a code module.

| Name | Data compression module |
| --- | --- |
| Purpose: | Code module for Huffman data compression Inputs Encoding table, uncoded byte-size input symbols Outputs Packed compressed output symbols |
| Functions | Huffman coding Performance Requires fast performance Manufacturing cost N/A |
| Power | N/A Physical size and weight N/A |

## Specification

Let's refine the description of Figure 3.20 to come up with a more complete specification for our data compression module. That collaboration diagram concentrates on the steady-state behavior of the system. For a fully functional system, we have to provide the following additional behavior.

- We have to be able to provide the compressor with a new symbol table.
- We should be able to flush the symbol buffer to cause the system to release all pending symbols that have been partially packed. We may want to do this when we change the symbol table or in the middle of an encoding session to keep a transmitter busy.

A class description for this refined understanding of the requirements on the module is shown in Figure 3.21. The class's buffer and current-bit behaviors keep track of the state of the encoding, and the table attribute provides the current symbol table. The class has three methods as follows:

- Encode performs the basic encoding function. It takes in a 1-byte input symbol and returns two values: a boolean showing whether it is returning a full buffer and, if the boolean is true, the full buffer itself
- New-symbol-table installs a new symbol table into the object and throws away the current contents of the internal buffer.

- Flush returns the current state of the buffer, including the number of valid bits in the buffer.

The *data-buffer* will be used to hold both packed symbols and unpacked ones (such as in the  symbol  table). It defines the buffer itself and the length of the buffer.  We  have to define a data  type because the  longest encoded symbol  is  longer  than  an  input symbol. The longest Huffman code for an eight-bit input symbol is 256 bits. (Ending  up with a symbol this long happens  only  when  the  symbol  probabilities  have  the  proper values.) The insert function packs a new  symbol  into  the  upper  bits  of the  buffer;  it  also puts the remaining bits in a new buffer if the  current  buffer  is  overflowed.  The *Symbol-table*  class   indexes

### *Program Design*

Since we  are only  building  an  encoder, the   program   is  fairly  simple. We will use this as an opportunity to compare object-oriented and non-OO implementations by coding  the design in both C++ and  C.

### *OO design in C++*

First is the object-oriented design  using  C++,  since  this  implementation  most  closely mirrors the  specification. The  first step  is to design  the data  buffer.  The  data  buffer needs to be as long as the longest symbol.  We  also  need  to  implement  a  function  that  lets  us merge  in another  data_buffer, shifting  the  incoming buffer  by the  proper amount.

```
const int databuflen = 8;  /* as long in  bytes as longest symbol
*/const int  bitsperbyte =  8;  /* definition  of byte */
const int  bytemask =  0xff;  /* use  to  mask  to  8 bits  for  safety */ const char  lowbitsmask
[bitsperbyte]  =  { 0,  1, 3,  7,  15,  31,63,  127};
/* used to keep low bits in a byte */
 typedef char boolean; /* for clarity   */
#define  TRUE 1
#define  FALSE 0
Class data_buffer  {
char databuf[databuflen];
int len;
int  length_in_chars() { return  len/bitsperbyte; }
/* length in bytes rounded down-used in implementation */
public:
void insert(data_buffer,  data_buffer&);
```

```cpp
int length() { return len; } /* returns number of bits in symbol */
int length_in_bytes() { return (int)ceil(len/8.0); }
void initialize(); /* initializes the data structure */
void data_buffer::fill(data_buffer, int);
/* puts upper bits of symbol into buffer */
data_buffer& operator=(data_buffer&);
/* assignment operator */
data_buffer() { initialize(); } /* C++ constructor */
~data_buffer() { } /* C++ destructor */
};
data_buffer empty_buffer; /* use this to initialize   other data_buffers */
void data_buffer::insert(data_buffer newval, data_buffer&
newbuf) {
/* This function puts the lower bits of a symbol (newval) into an existing    buffer    without
overflowing the  buffer. Puts spillover, if any, into newbuf. */
int i, j, bitstoshift, maxbyte;
/* precalculate  number  of positions to  shift up */
bitstoshift  =  length()   –  length_in_bytes()*bitsperbyte;
/* compute how many bytes to transfer–can't run past end of this buffer  */
maxbyte  =  newval.length()  +  length() >
databuflen*bitsperbyte ?
databuflen : newval.length_in_chars();
for (i  =  0;  i < maxbyte;  i++) {
/*  add lower bits of this  newval byte */
databuf[i + length_in_chars()] | = (newval.databuf[i] << bitstoshift) & byte-mask;
/*  add upper bits of this  newval byte */
databuf[i + length_in_chars() + 1] | = (newval.databuf[i] >> (bitsperbyte  –
bitstoshift))  &
lowbitsmask[bitsperbyte – bitstoshift];
}
/* fill  up  new buffer if  necessary */
if  (newval.length()  + length() > databuflen*bitsperbyte)    {
/* precalculate number  of positions to  shift down */
bitstoshift  = length() % bitsperbyte;
```

```cpp
for (i = maxbyte, j = 0; i++, j++;
i <= newval.length_in_chars())
{
newbuf.databuf[j] = (newval.databuf[i] >> bitstoshift) &bytemask;
newbuf.databuf[j]  | = newval.databuf[i +  1]   & lowbitsmask[bitstoshift];
}
}
/*  update length */
len = len + newval.length() > databuflen*bitsperbyte     ?
databuflen*bitsperbyte : len +
newval.length();
}
data_buffer& data_buffer::operator=(data_buffer& e) {
/* assignment operator for data buffer */ int  i;
/* copy the buffer itself   */   for (i = 0; i < databuflen; i++)
databuf[i]  = e.databuf[i];
/* set length */ len  = e.len;
/* return */ return e;
}
void data_buffer::fill(data_buffer  newval, int shiftamt) {
/*  This function puts the upper bits of a symbol (newval) into  the buffer. */
int i, bitstoshift, maxbyte;
/*  precalculate  number  of  positions to  shift up */
bitstoshift  =  length()  -  length_in_bytes()*bitsperbyte;
/* compute how many bytes to transfer-can't run past end of this buffer  */
maxbyte = newval.length_in_chars() > databuflen ?
databuflen : newval.length_in_chars();
for (i = 0;  i < maxbyte;  i++) {
/*  add lower bits of this  newval byte */
databuf[i + length_in_chars()] = newval.databuf[i] <<  bitstoshift;
/*  add upper bits of this  newval byte */
databuf[i + length_in_chars() + 1] =newval.databuf[i]  >>  (bitsperbyte   –
bitstoshift);
}
```

```cpp
}
void data_buffer::initialize()        {
/* Initialization  code for data_buffer. */
int i;
/* initializebuffer to all  zero bits */
for (i = 0; i < databuflen;  i++)
databuf[i]  = 0;
/* initialize length to zero */
len = 0;
}
```

The code for data_buffer is relatively  complex,  and  not  all  of  its  complexity  was reflected in the state diagram  of  Figure  3.25.  That  does  not  mean  the  specification  was bad, but only that it was written at a higher  level of abstraction.

The symbol table code can be implemented relatively  easily  as  shown  below. const  int nsymbols  =  256;

```cpp
Class symbol_table { data_buffer symbols[nsymbols]; public:
data_buffer value(int  i)
{
return symbols[i];
}
void load(symbol_table&);
symbol_table() { } /* C++ constructor */
~symbol_table() { } /* C++ destructor */
};
void symbol_table::load(symbol_table& newsyms) {
int i;
for (i = 0; i < nsymbols; i++)
{
symbols[i]  =  newsyms.symbols[i];
}
}
```

Now let's create the class definition for data_compressor: typedef  char  boolean;  /*
for clarity   */
class     data_compressor

```cpp
{
data_buffer buffer;
int current_bit;
symbol_table table;
public:
boolean encode(char, data_buffer&);
void new_symbol_table(symbol_table newtable)
{ table = newtable; current_bit     = 0;
buffer = empty_buffer;
} int flush(data_buffer& buf)
{ int temp = current_bit;
buf = buffer;
buffer = empty_buffer;
current_bit = 0;
return temp; }
data_compressor() { } /* C++ constructor */
~data_compressor() { } /* C++ destructor */
};
```

Now let's implement the encode( ) method.

The main challenge here is managing the buffer.

```cpp
boolean data_compressor::encode(char isymbol, data_buffer&
fullbuf)
{
data_buffer temp; int overlen;
/* look up the new symbol */
temp = table.value(isymbol); /* the symbol itself */
/* will this symbol overflow the buffer? */
overlen = temp.length() + current_bit –
buffer.length(); /* amount of overflow */
if ( overlen > 0 )
{
/* we did in fact overflow */
data_buffer nextbuf; buffer.insert(temp,nextbuf);
/* return the full buffer and keep the next partial buffer */
```

fullbuf = buffer; buffer = nextbuf; return  TRUE;

} else { /* no overflow */

data_buffer no_overflow; buffer.insert(temp,no_overflow);

/* won't use this argument */

if   (current_bit == buffer.length())

{

/* return current buffer */

fullbuf = buffer; buffer.initialize();/* initialize the buffer */return TRUE;

}

else return FALSE; /* buffer isn't  full  yet */

}

}

### *OO design in C*

How would we have to modify the implementation for C? We have two choices in implementation, based on whether we want to support multiple simultaneous data compressors. If we want to strictly adhere to the specification, we must be able to run several simultaneous compressors, since in the object-oriented specification we can create as many new data-compressor objects as we want. The fundamental point is that we cannot rely on any global variables—all of the object state must be replicable. We can do this relatively easily, making the code  only  a little more cumbersome. We create a structure that holds the data part of the object as  follows:

struct data_compressor_struct {

data_buffer buffer; int current_bit; sym_table table;

}

typedef struct  data_compressor_struct data_compressor,

*data_compressor_ptr; /* data type declaration for convenience */

We would, of course, have to do something similar for the other classes. Depend- ing on how strict we want to be, we may want  to define  data access functions to get to fields in the various structures we create. C would permit us to get to those struct fields  without using the access functions, but using the access functions would give us a little  extra freedom  to modify the structure definitions later. We then implement the class methods as C functions, passing in a pointer to the data_compressor object we want to operate on  Appearing below is the beginning of the modified encode method showing how we make explicit all references to the data in the object.

```c
typedef char boolean; /* for clarity   */
#define  TRUE 1
#define  FALSE 0
boolean  data_compressor_encode(data_compressor_ptr mycmprs, char isymbol, data_buffer
*fullbuf)
{
data_buffer temp; int len, overlen;
/* look up the new symbol */
temp = mycmprs->table[isymbol].value; /* the symbol itself*/
len = mycmprs->table[isymbol].length; /* its value */
...
```

(For C++ afficionados, the above amounts to making explicit the C++ this pointer.)

```c
static data_buffer buffer; static int current_bit; static sym_table table;
```

We have used the C static declaration to ensure that these globals are not defined outside the file in which they are defined; this gives us a little added modularity. We would, of course, have to update the specification so that it makes clear that only one compressor object can be running at a time. The functions that implement the methods can then operate directly on the globals as seen below.

```c
boolean data_compressor_encode(char isymbol, data_buffer*
fullbuf) {
data_buffer temp; int len, overlen;
/* look up the new symbol */
temp = table[isymbol].value; /* the symbol itself */
len = table[isymbol].length; /* its value */
...
```

Notice that this code does not need the structure pointer argument, making it resemble the C++ code a little more closely. However, horrible bugs will ensue if we try to run two different compressions at the same time through this code.

What can we say about the efficiency of this code? Efficiency has many aspects covered in more detail in Chapter 5. For the moment, let's consider instruction selection, that is, how well the compiler does in choosing the right instructions to implement the operations. Bit manipulations such as we do here often raise concerns about efficiency. But if we have a good compiler and we select the right data types, instruction selection is usually not a problem. If we use data types that do not require data type transformations, a good compiler can select the right instructions to efficiently implement the required operations.

### *Testing*

How do we test this program module to be sure it works? We consider testing much more thoroughly in Section 5.10. In the meantime, we can use common sense to come up with some testing techniques.

One way to test the code is to run it and look at the output without considering how the code is written. In this case, we can load up a symbol table, run some symbols through it, and see whether we get the correct result. We can get the symbol table from outside sources (such as the tables of Application Example 3.4)

Testing the internals of code often requires building scaffolding code. For example, we may want to test the insert method separately, which would require building a program that calls the method with the proper values. If our programming language comes with an interpreter, building such scaffolding is easier because we do not have to create a complete executable, but we often want to automate such tests even with interpreters because we will usually execute them several times

# Unit-3

## BUS-BASED COMPUTER SYSTEMS

## The CPU Bus

A computer system encompasses much more than the CPU; it also includes memory and I/O devices. The bus is the mechanism by which the CPU communicates with memory and devices. A bus is, at a minimum, a collection of wires, but the bus also defines a protocol by which the CPU, memory, and devices communicate. One of the major roles of the bus is to provide an interface to memory. (Of course, I/O devices also connect to the bus.) Based on understanding of the bus, we study the characteristics of memory components in this section.

### Bus Protocols

The basic building block of most bus protocols is the four-cycle handshake, illustrated in Figure 4.1. The handshake ensures that when two devices want to communicate, one is ready to transmit and the other is ready to receive. The hand- shake uses a pair of wires dedicated to the handshake: enq(meaning enquiry) and ack (meaning acknowledge). Extra wires are used for the data transmitted during the handshake. The four cycles are described below.

- Device 1 raises its output to signal an enquiry, which tells device 2 that it should get ready to listen for data.
- When device 2 is ready to receive, it raises its output to signal an acknowledgment. At this point, devices 1 and 2 can transmit or receive.
- Once the data transfer is complete, device 2 lowers its output, signaling that it has received the data.
- After seeing that ack has been released, device 1 lowers its output.

At the end of the handshake, both handshaking signals are low, just as they were at the start of the handshake. The system has thus returned to its original state in readiness for another handshake-enabled data transfer.

Microprocessor buses build on the handshake for communication between the CPU and other system components. The term bus is used in two ways. The most basic use is as a set of related wires, such as address wires. However, the term may also mean a protocol for communicating between components. To avoid confusion, we will use the term bundle to refer to a set of related signals. The fundamental bus operations are reading and writing. Figure 4.2

shows the structure of a typical bus that supports reads and writes. The major components follow:

- Clock provides synchronization to the bus components,
- R/W is true when the bus is reading and false when the bus is writing,
- Address is an a-bit bundle of signals that transmits the address for an access,
- Data is an n-bit bundle of signals that can carry data to or from the CPU, and
- Data ready signals when the values on the data bundle are valid.

All transfers on this basic bus are controlled by the CPU—the CPU can read or write a device or memory, but devices or memory cannot initiate a transfer. This is reflected by the fact that R/W and address are unidirectional signals, since only the CPU can determine the address and direction of the transfer.

The behavior of a bus is most often specified as a timing diagram. A timing diagram shows how the signals on a bus vary over time, but since values like the address and data can take on many values, some standard notation is used to describe signals, as shown in Figure 4.3. A's value is known at all times, so it is shown as a standard waveform that changes between zero and one. B and C alternate between changing and stable states. A stable signal has, as the name implies, a stable value that could be measured by an oscilloscope, but the exact value of that signal does not matter for purposes of the timing diagram. For exam- ple, an address bus may be shown as stable when the address is present, but the bus's timing requirements are independent of the exact address on the bus. A signal can go between a known 0/1 state and a stable/changing state. A changing signal does not have a stable value. Changing signals should not be used for computation. To be sure that signals go to their proper values at the proper times, timing diagrams sometimes show timing constraints. We draw timing constraints in two different ways, depending on whether we are concerned with the amount of time between events or only the order of events. The timing constraint from A to B, for example, shows that A must go high before B becomes stable. The constraint from A to B also has a time value of 10 ns, indicating that A goes high at least 10 ns before B goes stable.

Figure 3 .4 shows a timing diagram for the example bus. The diagram shows a read and a write. Timing constraints are shown only for the read operation, but similar constraints apply to the write operation.

The bus is normally in the read mode since that does not change the state of any of the devices or memories. The CPU can then ignore the bus data lines until it wants to use the results of a read. Notice also that the direction of data transfer on bidirectional lines is not specified in the timing diagram. During a read, the external device or memory is sending a value on the data lines, while during a write the CPU is controlling the data lines.

The sequence of operations for a read on the timing diagram as follows:

- A read or write is initiated by setting address enable high after the clock starts to rise. We set R/W 1 to indicate a read, and the address lines are set to the desired address.
- One clock cycle later, the memory or device is expected to assert the data value at that address on the data lines. Simultaneously, the external device specifies that the data are valid by pulling down the data ready line. This line is active low, meaning that a logically true value is indicated by a low voltage, in order to provide increased immunity to electrical noise.
- The CPU is free to remove the address at the end of the clock cycle and must do so before the beginning of the next cycle. The external device has a similar requirement for removing the data value from the data lines.

The write operation has a similar timing structure. The read/write sequence does illustrate that timing constraints are required on the transition of the R/W signal between read and write states. The signal must, of course, remain stable within a read or write. As a result there is a restricted time window in which the CPU can change between read and write modes.

The handshake that tells the CPU and devices when data are to be transferred is formed by data ready for the acknowledge side, but is implicit for the enquiry side. Since the bus is normally in read mode, enq does not need to be asserted, but the acknowledge must be provided by data ready.

The data ready signal allows the bus to be connected to devices that are slower than the bus. As shown in Figure 4.5, the external device need not immediately assert data ready. The cycles between the minimum time at which data can be asserted and when it is actually asserted are known as wait states. Wait states are commonly used to connect slow, inexpensive memories to buses.

We can also use the bus handshaking signals to perform burst transfers, as illustrated in Figure 4.6. In this burst read transaction, the CPU sends one address but receives a sequence of data values. We add an extra line to the bus, called burst9 here, which signals when a transaction is actually a burst. Releasing the burst9 signal tells the device that enough data has been transmitted. To stop receiving data after the end of data 4, the CPU releases the burst9 signal at the end of data 3 since the device requires some time to recognize the end of the burst. Those values come from successive memory locations starting at the given address.

Some buses provide disconnected transfers. In these buses, the request and response are separate. A first operation requests the transfer. The bus can then be used for other operations. The transfer is completed later, when the data are ready.

The state machine view of the bus transaction is also helpful and a useful complement to the timing diagram. Figure 4.7 shows the CPU and device state machines forthe read operation. As with a timing diagram, we do not show all the possible values of address and data lines but instead concentrate on the transitions of control signals. When the CPU decides to perform a read transaction, it moves to a new state, sending bus signals that cause the device to behave appropriately. The device's state transition graph captures its side of the protocol.

Some buses have data bundles that are smaller than the natural word size of the CPU. Using fewer data lines reduces the cost of the chip. Such buses are easiest to design when the CPU is natively addressable. A more complicated protocol hides the smaller data sizes from the instruction execution unit in the CPU. Byte addresses are sequentially sent over the bus, receiving one byte at a time; the bytes are assembled inside the CPU's bus logic before being presented to the CPU proper.

Some buses use multiplexed address and data. As shown in Figure 4.8, additional control lines are provided to tell whether the value on the address/data lines is an address or data. Typically, the address comes first on the combined address/data lines, followed by the data. The address can be held in a register until the data arrive so that both can be presented to the device (such as a RAM) at the same time.

## DMA

Standard bus transactions require the CPU to be in the middle of every read and write transaction. However, there are certain types of data transfers in which the CPU does not need to be involved. For example, a high-speed I/O device may want to transfer a block of data into memory. While it is possible to write a program that alternately reads the device and writes to memory, it would be faster to eliminate the CPU's involvement and let the device and memory communicate directly. This Direct memory access (DMA) is a bus operation that allows reads and writes not controlled by the CPU. A DMA transfer is controlled by a DMA controller, which requests control of the bus from the CPU. After gaining control, the DMA controller performs read and write operations directly between devices and memory.

Figure 4.9 shows the configuration of a bus with a DMA controller. The DMA requires the CPU to provide two additional bus signals:

- The bus request is an input to the CPU through which DMA controllers ask for ownership of the bus.
- The bus grant signals that the bus has been granted to the DMA controller.

A device that can initiate its own bus transfer is known as a bus master. Devices that do not have the capability to be bus masters do not need to connect to a bus request and bus grant. The DMA controller uses these two signals to gain control of the bus using a classic four-cycle handshake. The bus request is asserted by the DMA controller when it wants to control the bus, and the bus grant is asserted by the CPU when the bus is ready.

The CPU will finish all pending bus transactions before granting control of the bus to the DMA controller. When it does grant control, it stops driving the other bus signals: R/W, address, and so on. Upon becoming bus master, the DMA con- troller has control of all bus signals (except, of course, for bus request and bus grant).

Once the DMA controller is bus master, it can perform reads and writes using the same bus protocol as with any CPU-driven bus transaction. Memory and devices do not know whether a read or write is performed by the CPU or by a DMA controller. After the transaction is finished, the DMA controller returns the bus to the CPU by deasserting the bus request, causing the CPU to deassert the bus grant.

The CPU controls the DMA operation through registers in the DMA controller. A typical DMA controller includes the following three registers:

- A starting address register specifies where the transfer is to begin.
- A length register specifies the number of words to be transferred.
- A status register allows the DMA controller to be operated by the CPU.

The CPU initiates a DMA transfer by setting the starting address and length registers appropriately and then writing the status register to set its start transfer bit. After the DMA operation is complete, the DMA controller interrupts the CPU to tell it that the transfer is done. What is the CPU doing during a DMA transfer? It cannot use the bus. As illustrated in Figure 4.10, if the CPU has enough instructions and data in the cache and registers, it may be able to continue doing useful work for quite some time and may not notice the DMA transfer. But once the CPU needs the bus, it stalls until the DMA controller returns bus mastership to the CPU. To prevent the CPU from idling for too long, most DMA controllers implement modes that occupy the bus for only a few cycles at a time. For example, the transfer may be made 4, 8, or 16 words at a time. As illustrated in Figure 4.11, after each block, the DMA controller returns control of the bus to the CPU and goes to sleep for a preset period, after which it requests the bus again for the next block transfer.

### *System Bus Configurations*

A microprocessor system often has more than one bus. As shown in Figure 4.12, high- speed devices may be connected to a high-performance bus,while lower-speed devices are connected to a different bus. A small block of logic known as a bridge allows the buses to connect to each other. There are several good reasons to use multiple buses and bridges:

- Higher-speed buses may provide wider data connections.
- A high-speed bus usually requires more expensive circuits and connectors. The cost of low-speed devices can be held down by using a lower-speed, lower-cost bus.

The bridge may allow the buses to operate independently, thereby providing some parallelism in I/O operations. In Section 4.5.3, we see that PCs often use this methodology.

Let's consider the operation of a bus bridge between what we will call a fast bus and a slow bus as illustrated in Figure 4.13. The bridge is a slave on the fast bus and the master of the slow bus. The bridge takes commands from the fast bus on which it is a slave and issues those commands on the slow bus. It also returns the results from the slow bus to the fast bus— for example, it returns the results of a read on the slow bus to the fast bus.

The upper sequence of states handles a write from the fast bus to the slow bus. These states must read the data from the fast bus and set up the handshake for the slow bus. Operations on the fast and slow sides of the bus bridge should be overlapped as much as possible to reduce the latency of bus-to-bus transfers. Similarly, the bottom sequence of states reads from the slow bus and writes the data to the fast bus.

The bridge serves as a protocol translator between the two bridges as well. If the bridges are very close in protocol operation and speed, a simple state machine may be enough. If there are larger differences in the protocol and timing between the two buses, the bridge may need to use registers to hold some data values temporarily.

## AMBA Bus

Since the ARM CPU is manufactured by many different vendors, the bus provided off- chip can vary from chip to chip. ARM has created a separate bus specification for single-chip systems. The AMBA bus [ARM99A] supports CPUs, memories, and peripherals integrated in a system-on-silicon. As shown in Figure 4.14, the AMBA specification includes two buses. The

AMBA high-performance bus (AHB) is optimized for high-speed transfers and is directly connected to the CPU. It supports several high-performance features: pipelining, burst transfers, split transactions, and multiple bus masters.

A bridge can be used to connect the AHB to an AMBA peripherals bus (APB). This bus is designed to be simple and easy to implement; it also consumes relatively little power. The AHB assumes that all peripherals act as slaves, simplifying the logic required in both the peripherals and the bus controller. It also does not perform pipelined operations, which simplifies the bus logic.

## Memory Devices

In this section, we introduce the basic types of memory components that are com- monly used in embedded systems. Now that we understand the operation of the bus, we are able to understand the pinouts of these memories and how values are read and written. We also need to understand the varieties of memory cells that are used to build memories. There are several varieties of both read-only and read/write memories, each with its own advantages. After discussing some basic characteristics of memories, we describe RAMs and then ROMs.

### *Memory Device Organization*

The most basic way to characterize a memory is by its capacity, such as 256 MB. However, manufacturers usually make several versions of a memory of a given size, each with a different data width. For example, a 256-MB memory may be available in two versions:

- As a 64 M 4-bit array, a single memory access obtains an 8-bit data item, with a maximum of $2^{26}$ different addresses.

- As a 32 M 8-bit array, a single memory access obtains a 1-bit data item, with a maximum of $2^{23}$ different addresses.

The height/width ratio of a memory is known as its aspect ratio. The best aspect ratio depends on the amount of memory required. Internally, the data are stored in a two-dimensional array of memory cells as shown in Figure 4.15. Because the array is stored in two dimensions, the n-bit address received by the chip is split into a row and a column address (with n r c). The row and column select a particular memory cell. If the memory's external width is 1 bit, the column address selects a single bit; for wider data widths, the column address can be used to select a subset of the columns. Most memories include an enable signal that controls the tri-stating of data onto the memory's pins. We will see in Section 4.4.1 how the enable pin can be used to easily build large memories from multiple banks of memory chips. A read/write signal (R/W in the figure) on read/write memories controls the direction of data transfer; memory chips do not typically have separate read and write data pins.

### Random-Access Memories

Random-access memories can be both read and written. They are called random access because, unlike magnetic disks, addresses can be read in any order. Most bulk memory in modern systems is dynamic RAM (DRAM). DRAM is very dense; it does, however, require that its values be refreshed periodically since the values inside the memory cells decay over time.

The dominant form of dynamic RAM today is the synchronous DRAMs (SDRAMs), which uses clocks to improve DRAM performance.

SDRAMs use Row Address Select (RAS) and Column Address Select (CAS) signals to break the address into two parts, which select the proper row and column in the RAM array. Signal transitions are relative to the SDRAM clock, which allows the internal SDRAM operations to be pipelined. As shown in Figure 4.16, transitions on the control signals are related to a clock [Mic00]. RAS and CAS can therefore become valid at the same time.

The address lines are not shown in full detail here; some address lines may not be active depending on the mode in use. SDRAMs use a separate refresh signal to control refreshing. DRAM has to be refreshed roughly once per millisecond.

Rather than refresh the entire memory at once, DRAMs refresh part of the memory at a time. When a section of memory is being refreshed, it cannot be accessed until the refresh is complete. The memory refresh occurs over fairly few seconds so that each section is refreshed every few microseconds.

SDRAMs include registers that control the mode in which the SDRAM operates. SDRAMs support burst modes that allow several sequential addresses to be accessed by sending only one address.

SDRAMs generally also support an interleaved mode that exchanges pairs of bytes.

Even faster synchronous DRAMs, known as double-data rate (DDR) SDRAMs or DDR2 and DDR3 SDRAMs, are now in use.

The details of DDR operation are beyond the scope of this book, but the basic capabilities of DDR memories are similar to those of single-rate SDRAMs; DDRs simply use sophisticated circuit techniques to perform more operations per clock cycle.

### *SIMMs and DIMMs*

Memory for PCs is generally purchased as single in-line memory modules (SIMMs) or double in-line memory modules (DIMMs). A SIMM or DIMM is a small circuit board that fits into a standard memory socket. A DIMM has two sets of leads compared to the SIMM's one. Memory chips are soldered to the circuit board to supply the desired memory.

### *Read-Only Memories*

Read-only memories (ROMs) are pre-programmed with fixed data. They are very useful in embedded systems since a great deal of the code, and perhaps some data, does not change over time. Read-only memories are also less sensitive to radiation-induced errors.

There are several varieties of ROM available.

The first-level distinction to be made is between factory-programmed ROM (sometimes called mask-programmed ROM) and field-programmable ROM.

Factory-programmed ROMs are ordered from the factory with particular programming. ROMs can typically be ordered in lots of a few thousand, but clearly factory programming is useful only when the ROMs are to be installed in some quantity.

Field-programmable ROMs, on the other hand, can be programmed in the lab. Flash memory is the dominant form of field-programmable ROM and is electrically erasable.

Flash memory uses standard system voltage for erasing and programming, allowing it to be reprogrammed inside a typical system. This allows applications such as automatic distribution of upgrades—the flash memory can be reprogrammed while downloading the new memory contents from a telephone line.

Early flash memories had to be erased in their entirety; modern devices allow memory to be erased in blocks. Most flash memories today allow certain blocks to be protected.

## I/O Devices

In this section we survey some input and output devices commonly used in embed- ded computing systems. Some of these devices are often found as on-chip devices in micro-controllers; others are generally implemented separately but are still commonly used.

Looking at a few important devices now will help us understand both the requirements of device interfacing in this chapter and the uses of devices in programming in this and later chapters.

### Timers and Counters

Timers and counters are distinguished from one another largely by their use, not their logic. Both are built from adder logic with registers to hold the current value, with an increment input that adds one to the current register value.

A timer has its count connected to a periodic clock signal to measure time intervals, while a counter has its count input connected to an a periodic signal in order to count the number of occurrences of some external event. Because the same logic can be used for either purpose, the device is often called a counter/timer.

Figure 4.17 shows enough of the internals of a counter/timer to illustrate its operation. An n-bit counter/timer uses an n-bit register to store the current state of the count and an array of half subtractors to decrement the count when the count signal is asserted. Combinational logic checks when the count equals zero; the done output signals the zero count. It is often useful to be able to control the time-out, rather than require exactly 2n events to occur. For this purpose, a reset register provides the value with which the count register is to be loaded. The counter/timer provides logic to load the reset register. Most counters provide both cyclic and acyclic modes of operation. In the cyclic mode, once the counter reaches the done state, it is automatically reloaded and the counting process continues. In acyclic mode, the counter/timer waits for an explicit signal from the microprocessor to resume counting.

A watchdog timer is an I/O device that is used for internal operation of a system. As shown in Figure 4.18, the watchdog timer is connected into the CPU bus and also to the CPU's reset line. The CPU's software is designed to periodically reset the watchdog timer, before the timer ever reaches its time-out limit. If the watchdog timer ever does reach that limit, its time-out action is to reset the processor. In that case, the presumption is that either a software flaw or hardware problem has caused the CPU to misbehave. Rather than diagnose the problem, the system is reset to get it operational as quickly as possible.

### A/D and D/A Converters

Analog/digital (A/D) and digital/analog (D/A) converters (typically known as ADCs and DACs, respectively) are often used to interface nondigital devices to embedded systems. The design of A/D and D/A converters themselves is beyond the scope of this book; we concentrate instead on the interface to the micropro- cessor bus. Because A/D conversion requires more complex circuitry, it requires a somewhat more complex interface. Analog/digital conversion requires sampling the analog input before converting it to digital form. A control signal causes the A/D converter to take a sample and digitize it.

There are several different types of A/D converter circuits, some of which take a constant amount of time, while the conversion time of others depends on the sampled value. Variable-time converters provide a done signal so that the microprocessor knows when the value is ready. A typical A/D interface has, in addition to its analog inputs, two major digital inputs. A data port allows A/D registers to be read and written, and a clock input tells when to start the next conversion.

D/A conversion is relatively simple, so the D/A converter interface generally includes only the data value. The input value is continuously converted to analog form.

### Keyboards

A keyboard is basically an array of switches, but it may include some internal logic to help simplify the interface to the microprocessor. In this chapter, we build our understanding from a single switch to a microprocessor-controlled keyboard A hardware debouncing circuit can be built using a one-shot timer. Software can also be used to debounce switch inputs. A raw keyboard can be assembled from several switches. Each switch in a raw keyboard has its own pair of terminals, making raw keyboards impractical when a large number of keys is required.

The microprocessor can provide debouncing, but it also provides other functions as well. An encoded keyboard uses some code to represent which switch is currently being depressed. At the heart of the encoded keyboard is the scanned array of switches shown in Figure 4.20. Unlike a raw keyboard, the scanned keyboard array reads only one row of switches at a time. The demultiplexer at the left side of the array selects the row to be read. When the scan input is 1, that value is transmitted to one terminal of each key in the row. If the switch is depressed, the 1 is sensed at that switch's column. Since only one switch in the column is activated, that value uniquely identifies a key. The row address and column output can be used for encoding, or circuitry can be used to give a different encoding.

A consequence of encoding the keyboard is that combinations of keys may not be represented. For example, on a PC keyboard, the encoding must be chosen so that combinations such as control-Q can be recognized and sent to the PC. Another consequence is that rollover may not be allowed. For example, if you press "a," and then press "b" before releasing "a," in most applications you want the keyboard to send an "a" followed by a "b." Rollover is very common in typing at even modest rates. A naive implementation of the encoder circuitry will simply throw away any character depressed after the first one until all the keys are released. The keyboard microcontroller can be programmed to provide n-key rollover, so that rollover keys are sensed, put on a stack, and transmitted in sequence as keys are released.

## LEDs

Light-emitting diodes (LEDs) are often used as simple displays by themselves, and arrays of LEDs may form the basis of more complex displays. Figure 4.21 shows how to connect an LED to a digital output. A resistor is connected between the output pin and the LED to absorb the voltage difference between the digital output voltage and the 0.7 V drop across the LED. When the digital output goes to 0, the LED voltage is in the device's off region and the LED is not on.

### *Displays*

A display device may be either directly driven or driven from a frame buffer. Typically, displays with a small number of elements are driven directly by logic, while large displays use a RAM frame buffer.

The n-digit array, shown in Figure 4.22, is a simple example of a display that is usually directly driven. A single-digit display typically consists of seven segments; each segment may be either an LED or a liquid crystal display (LCD) element. This display relies on the digits being visible for some time after the drive to the digit is removed, which is true for both LEDs and LCDs. The digit input is used to choose which digit is currently being updated, and the selected digit activates its display elements based on the current data value. The display's driver is responsible for repeatedly scanning through the digits and presenting the current value of each to the display.

A frame buffer is a RAM that is attached to the system bus. The microprocessor writes values into the frame buffer in whatever order is desired. The pixels in the frame buffer are generally written to the display in raster order (by tradition, the screen is in the fourth quadrant) by reading pixels sequentially.

Many large displays are built using LCD. Each pixel in the display is formed by a single liquid crystal. LCD displays present a very different interface to the system because the array of pixel LCDs can be randomly accessed. Early LCD panels were called passive matrix because they relied on a two-dimensional grid of wires to address the pixels. Modern LCD panels use an active matrix system that puts a transistor at each pixel to control access to the LCD. Active matrix displays provide higher contrast and a higher-quality display

### *Touchscreens*

A touchscreen is an input device overlaid on an output device. The touchscreen registers the position of a touch to its surface. By overlaying this on a display, the user can react to information shown on the display.

The two most common types of touchscreens are resistive and capacitive. A resistive touchscreen uses a two-dimensional voltmeter to sense position. As shown in Figure 4.23, the touchscreen consists of two conductive sheets separated by spacer balls. The top conductive sheet is flexible so that it can be pressed to touch the bottom sheet. A voltage is applied across the sheet; its resistance causes a voltage gradient to appear across the sheet. The top sheet samples the conductive sheet's applied voltage at the contact point. An analog/digital converter is used to measure the voltage and resulting position. The touchscreen alternates between x and y position sensing by alternately applying horizontal and vertical voltage gradients.

## Component Interfacing

Building the logic to interface a device to a bus is not too difficult but does take some attention to detail. We first consider interfacing memory components to the bus, since that is relatively simple, and then use those concepts to interface to other types of devices.

### *Memory Interfacing*

If we can buy a memory of the exact size we need, then the memory structure is simple. If we need more memory than we can buy in a single chip, then we must construct the memory out of several chips. We may also want to build a memory that is wider than we can buy on a single chip; for example, we cannot generally buy a 32- bit-wide memory chip. We can easily construct a memory of a given width (32 bits, 64 bits, etc.) by placing RAMs in parallel.

### *Device Interfacing*

Some I/O devices are designed to interface directly to a particular bus, forming glueless interfaces. But glue logic is required when a device is connected to a bus for which it is not designed.

An I/O device typically requires a much smaller range of addresses than a memory, so addresses must be decoded much more finely. Some additional logic is required to cause the bus to read and write the device's registers.

# Designing with Microprocessors

In this section we concentrate on how to create an initial working embedded system and how to ensure that the system works properly. Section 4.5.1 considers possible architectures for embedded computing systems. Section 3.5.2 studies techniques for designing the hardware components of embedded systems. Section 4.5.3 describes the use of the PC as an embedded computing platform.

## *System Architecture*

We know that an architecture is a set of elements and the relationships between them that together form a single unit. The architecture of an embedded computing system is the blueprint for implementing that system—it tells you what components you need and how you put them together. The architecture of an embedded computing system includes both hardware and software elements. Let's consider each in turn.

The hardware architecture of an embedded computing system is the more obvi- ous manifestation of the architecture since you can touch it and feel it. It includes several elements, some of which may be less obvious than others.

- **CPU** An embedded computing system clearly contains a microprocessor. But which one? There are many different architectures, and even within an architecture we can select between models that vary in clock speed, bus data width, integrated peripherals, and so on. The choice of the CPU is one of the most important, but it cannot be made without considering the software that will execute on the machine.
- **Bus** The choice of a bus is closely tied to that of a CPU, since the bus is an integral part of the microprocessor
- **Memory** Once again, the question is not whether the system will have memory but the characteristics of that memory. The most obvious characteristic is total size, which depends on both the required data volume and the size of the program instructions. The ratio of ROM to RAM and selection of DRAM versus SRAM can have a significant influence on the cost of the system. The speed of the memory will play a large part in determining system performance.
- **Input and output devices** The user's view of the input and output mechanisms may not correspond to the devices connected to the microprocessor. For example, a set of switches and knobs on a front panel may all be controlled by a single microcontroller, which is in turn connected to the main CPU. For a given function, there

may be several different devices of varying sophistication and cost that can do the job. The difficulty of using a particular device, such as the amount of glue logic required to interface it, may also play a role in final device selection.

You may not think of programs as having architectures, but well-designed programs do have structure that represents an architecture. A fundamental task in software architecture design is partitioning —breaking the functionality into pieces in a way that makes it easy to implement, test, and modify.

Most embedded systems will do more than one thing—for example, processing streams of data and handling the user interface. Mixing together different types of functionality into a single code module leads to spaghetti code, which has poorly structured control flow, excessive use of global data, and generally unreliable programs.

Breaking the system's functionality into pieces that roughly correspond to the major modes of operation and functions of the device is often a good choice. First, different types of functionality often require different programming styles, so that they will naturally fall into different procedures in the code. Second, the functionality boundaries often correspond to performance requirements. Since at least some of the software components will almost certainly have to finish executing within a given deadline, it is important to be able to identify the code that must satisfy the deadline and to measure the performance of that code.

It is also important to remember that some of the functionality may in fact be implemented in the I/O devices. You may have a choice between using a simple, inexpensive device that requires more software support or a more sophisticated and expensive device that can perform more functions automatically. (An example in the digital audio domain is -law scaling, which can be done automatically by some analog/digital converters.) Using DMA to move data rather than a programmed loop is another example of using hardware to substitute for software. Most of the functionality will be in the software, but careful consideration of the hardware architecture can help simplify the software and make it easier for the software to meet its performance requirements.

### Hardware Design

The design complexity of the hardware platform can vary greatly, from a totally off- the-shelf solution to a highly customized design. At the board level, the first step is to consider evaluation boards supplied by the microprocessor manufacturer or another company working in collaboration with the manufacturer. Evaluation boards are sold for many microprocessor systems; they typically include the CPU, some memory, a serial link for downloading programs, and some minimal number of I/O devices. Figure 4.24 shows an ARM evaluation board manufactured by Sharp. The evaluation board may be a complete solution or provide what you need with only slight modifications. If the evaluation board is supplied by the microprocessor vendor, its design (netlist, board layout, etc.) may be available from the vendor; companies provide such information to make it easy for customers to use their microprocessors. If the evaluation board comes from a third party, it may be possible to contract them to design a new board with your required modifications, or you can start from scratch on a new board design.

The other major task is the choice of memory and peripheral components. In the case of I/O devices, there are two alternatives for each device: selecting a component from a catalog or designing one yourself. When shopping for devices from a catalog, it is important to read data sheets carefully—it may not be trivial to figure out whether the device does what you need it to do. You should also consider the amount of glue logic required to connect the device to your bus. Simple peripheral logic can be implemented in programmable logic devices (PLDs), while more complex units can be built from field-programmable gate arrays (FPGAs).

### *The PC as a Platform*

Personal computers are often used as platforms for embedded computing. A PC offers several important advantages—it is a predesigned hardware platform with a great many features, a wide variety of I/O devices can be purchased for it, and it provides a rich programming environment. Because a PC-based system does not use custom hardware, it also carries the resulting disadvantages. It is larger, more power- hungry, and more expensive than a custom hardware platform would be. However, for low-volume applications and environments such as factories and offices where size and power are not critical,using a PC to build an embedded system often makes a lot of sense.The term personal computer has come to apply to a variety of machines, including IBM- compatibles, Macs, and others. In this section, we describe a generic PC architecture with some discussion of features relevant to different types of PCs. A detailed discussion of any of these platforms is beyond the scope of this book.

As shown in Figure 4.25, a typical PC includes several major hardware components:

- The CPU provides basic computational facilities.
- RAM is used for program storage.
- ROM holds the boot program.
- A DMA controller provides DMA capabilities.

- Timers are used by the operating system for a variety of purposes.
- A high-speed bus, connected to the CPU bus through a bridge, allows fast devices to communicate efficiently with the rest of the system.
- A low-speed bus provides an inexpensive way to connect simpler devices and may be necessary for backward compatibility as well.

PCI (Peripheral Component Interconnect) is the dominant high-performance system bus today. PCI uses high-speed data transmission techniques and efficient protocols to achieve high throughput. The original PCI standard allowed operation up to 33 MHz; at that rate, it could achieve a maximum transfer rate of 264 MB/s using 64-bit transfers. The revised PCI standard allows the bus to run up to 66 MHz, giving a maximum transfer rate of 524 MB/s with 64-bit wide transfers.

PCI uses wide buses with many data and address bits along with multiple control bits. The width of the bus both increases the cost of an interface to the bus and makes the physical connection to the bus more complicated. As a result, PC manufacturers have introduced serial buses to provide high-speed transfers while keeping the cost of connecting to the bus relatively low. USB (Universal Serial Bus) and IEEE 1394 are the two major high-speed serial buses. Both of these buses offer high transfer rates using simple connectors. They also allow devices to be chained together so that users don't have to worry about the order of devices on the bus or other details of connection.

A PC also provides a standard software platform that provides interfaces to the underlying hardware as well as more advanced services. At the bottom of the soft- ware platform structure in most PCs is a minimal set of software in ROM. This software is designed to load the complete operating system from some other device (disk, network, etc.), and it may also provide low-level hardware interfaces. In the IBM- compatible PC, the low-level software is known as the basic input/output system (BIOS). The BIOS provides low-level hardware drivers as well as booting facilities. The operating system provides high-level drivers, control of executing processes, user interfaces, and so on. Because the PC software environment is so rich, developing embedded code for a PC target is much easier than when a host must be connected to a CPU in a development target. However, if the software is delivered directly on a standard version of the operating system, the resulting software pack- age will require significant amounts of RAM as well as occupy a large disk image. Developers often create pared down versions of the operating system for delivering embedded code on PC platforms. Both the IBM-compatible PC and the Mac provide a combination of hardware and software that allows devices to provide their own configuration information. On the IBM-compatible PC, this is known as the Plug-and-Play standard developed by Microsoft. These standards make it possible to plug in a device and have it work directly, without hardware or software intervention from the user.

## Development and Debugging

In this section we take a step back from the platform and consider how it is used during design. We first consider how we can build an effective means for programming and testing an embedded system using hosts. We then see how hosts and other techniques can be used for debugging embedded systems.

### *Development Environments*

A typical embedded computing system has a relatively small amount of everything, including CPU horsepower, memory, I/O devices, and so forth. As a result, it is common to do at least part of the software development on a PC or workstation known as a host as illustrated in Figure 4.26. The hardware on which the code will finally run is known as the target . The host and target are frequently connected by a USB link, but a higher-speed link such as Ethernet can also be used. The target must include a small amount of software to talk to the host system. That software will take up some memory, interrupt vectors, and so on, but it should generally leave the smallest possible footprint in the target to avoid interfering with the application software. The host should be able to do the following:

- load programs into the target,
- start and stop program execution on the target, and
- examine memory and CPU registers.

A cross-compiler is a compiler that runs on one type of machine but generates code for another. After compilation, the executable code is downloaded to the embedded system by a serial link or perhaps burned in a PROM and plugged in. We also often make use of host-target debuggers,in which the basic hooks for debugging are provided by the target and a more sophisticated user interface is created by the host. A PC or workstation offers a programming environment that is in many ways much friendlier than the typical embedded computing platform. But one problem with this approach emerges when debugging code talks to I/O devices. Since the host almost certainly will not have the same devices configured in the same way, the embedded code cannot be run as is on the host. In many cases, a test- bench program can be built to help debug the embedded code. The testbench generates inputs to simulate the actions of the input devices; it may also take the output values and compare them against expected values, providing valuable early debugging help. The embedded code may need to be slightly modified to work with the testbench, but careful coding (such as using the #ifdef directive in C) can ensure that the changes can be undone easily and without introducing bugs.

### Debugging Techniques

A good deal of software debugging can be done by compiling and executing the code on a PC or workstation. But at some point it inevitably becomes necessary to run code on the embedded hardware platform. Embedded systems are usually less friendly programming environments than PCs. Nonetheless, the resourceful designer has several options available for debugging the system.

The serial port found on most evaluation boards is one of the most important debugging tools. In fact, it is often a good idea to design a serial port into an embedded system even if it will not be used in the final product; the serial port can be used not only for development debugging but also for diagnosing problems in the field. Another very important debugging tool is the breakpoint. The simplest form of a breakpoint is for the user to specify an address at which the program's execution is to break. When the PC reaches that address, control is returned to the monitor program. From the monitor program, the user can examine and/or modify CPU registers, after which execution can be continued. Implementing breakpoints does not require using exceptions or external devices.

### Programming Example 3.1

### Breakpoints

A breakpoint is a location in memory at which a program stops executing and returns to the debugging tool or monitor program. Implementing breakpoints is very simple—you simply replace the instruction at the breakpoint location with a subroutine call to the monitor. In the following code, to establish a breakpoint at location 0x40c in some ARM code, we've replaced the branch (B) instruction normally held at that location with a subroutine call (BL) to the breakpoint handling routine:

## System-Level Performance Analysis

Bus-based systems add another layer of complication to performance analysis. The CPU, bus, and memory or I/O device all act as independent elements that can operate in parallel. In this section, we will develop some basic techniques for analyzing the performance of bus-based systems.

### *System-Level Performance Analysis*

System-level performance involves much more than the CPU. We often focus on the CPU because it processes instructions, but any part of the system can affect total system performance. More precisely, the CPU provides an upper bound on performance, but any other part of the system can slow down the CPU. Merely counting instruction execution times is not enough. Consider the simple  system of Figure 4.28. We want  to move data from memory to the CPU to process it. To get the data from memory to the CPU we must:

- read from the memory;
- transfer over the bus to the cache; and
- transfer from the cache to the CPU.

The most basic measure of performance we are interested in is bandwidth— the rate at which we can move data. Ultimately, if we are interested in real-time performance, we are interested in real-time performance measured in seconds. But often the simplest way to measure performance is in units of clock cycles. However, different parts of the system will  run at different  clock  rates. We have to make sure that we apply the right clock rate to each part of the performance estimate when we convert from clock  cycles to seconds.

Bandwidth questions often come up when we are transferring  large blocks of data. For simplicity, let's  start  by  considering  the  bandwidth  provided  by  only one system component, the bus. Consider an image of 320 240 pixels, with each  pixel composed of  3 bytes of data. This gives a grand total of 230, 400 bytes of data. If these images are video frames, we want  to check if we  can push  one frame through the system within the 1/30 s that we have to process a frame before the next one arrives.

Let us assume that we can transfer one byte of data every  microsecond,  which implies a bus speed  of 1 MHz. In this case, we  would  require 230, 400  s  0.23   s to transfer one frame. That is more than  the  0.033  s  allotted  to  the  data  transfer. We  would  have  to increase  the  transfer  rate  by  7  to  satisfy  our  performance requirement.

We can increase bandwidth in two ways: We can increase the  clock rate of the bus or we can increase the amount of  data  transferred  per  clock cycle. For example, if we increased the bus to carry four  bytes  or  32  bits  per  transfer, we  would  reduce the transfer time to 0.058 s. If we could also increase the  bus clock rate to 2 MHz, then we would  reduce the transfer  time  to 0.029  s, which is within our  time  budget for  the transfer. How do we know how long it takes to transfer one  unit  of data?  To determine that, we have  to  look  at  the data  sheet  for the bus. As we saw in Section 4.1.1, a bus transfer generally takes more than one bus cycle. Burst transfers, which move to contiguous locations, may be more efficient per byte. We also need to know the width of the bus—how many bytes per transfer. Finally, we need to know the bus clock period, which in general will be different from the CPU clock period. Let's call the bus clock period P and the bus width W . We will put W of bytes but we could use other measures of width as well. We want to write for-our basic mauls for the time required to transfer N bytes of data. We will write counts to real formulas in units of bus cycles T , then convert those bus cycle time t using the bus clock period P :

A basic bus transfer transfers a W -wide set of bytes. The data transfer itself takes D clock cycles. (Ideally, D 1, but a memory that introduces wait states is one example of a transfer that could require D 1 cycles.)

### *System Architecture*

The software and hardware architectures of a system are always hard to completely separate, but let's first consider the software architecture and then its implications on the hardware. The system has both periodic and a periodic components—the current time must obviously be updated periodically, and the button commands occur occasionally. It seems reasonable to have the following two major software components:

- An interrupt-driven routine can update the current time. The current time will be kept in a variable in memory. A timer can be used to interrupt periodically and update the time. As seen in the subsequent discussion of the hardware

### *Component Design and Testing*

The two major software components, the interrupt handler and the foreground code, can be implemented relatively straightforwardly. Since most of the functionality of the interrupt handler is in the interruption process itself, that code is best tested on the microprocessor platform. The foreground code can be more easily tested on the PC or workstation used for code development.

### *System Integration and Testing*

Because this system has a small number of components, system integration is relatively easy. The software must be checked to ensure that debugging code has been turned off. Three types of tests can be performed. First, the clock's accuracy can be checked against a reference clock. Second, the commands can be exercised from the buttons. Finally, the buzzer's functionality should be verified.

# Unit-4

## Program Design and Analysis

### Stream-Oriented Programming and Circular Buffers

The data stream style makes sense for data that comes in regularly and must be processed on the fly. The FIR filter of Example 2.5 is a classic example of stream- oriented processing. For each sample, the filter must emit one output that depends on the values of the last n inputs. In a typical workstation application, we would process the samples over a given interval by reading them all in from a file and then computing the results all at once in a batch process. In an embedded system we must not only emit outputs in real time, but we must also do so using a minimum amount of memory. The circular buffer is a data structure that lets us handle streaming data in an efficient way. Figure 5.1 illustrates how a circular buffer stores a subset of the data stream. At each point in time, the algorithm needs a subset of the data stream that forms a window into the stream. The window slides with time as we throw out old values no longer needed and add new values. Since the size of the window does not

### Programming Example 4.2

### A circular buffer implementation of an FIR filter

Appearing below are the declarations for the circular buffer and filter coefficients, assuming that N , the number of taps in the filter, has been previously defined.

int circ_buffer[N]; /* circular buffer for data */

int circ_buffer_head = 0; /* current head of the buffer */

int c[N]; /* filter coefficients (constants) */

To write C code for a circular buffer-based FIR filter, we need to modify the original loop slightly. Because the 0th element of data may not be in the 0th element of the circular buffer, we have to change the way in which we access the data. One of the implications of this is that we need separate loop indices for the circular buffer and coefficients.

int f, /* loop counter */

ibuf, /* loop index for the circular buffer */ ic;        /* loop index for the coefficient array */ for (f = 0, ibuf = circ_buffer_head, ic = 0; ic < N;

ibuf = (ibuf == (N – 1) ? 0 : ibuf++),ic++) f = f + c[ic] * circ_buffer[ibuf];

The above code assumes that some other code, such as an interrupt handler, is replacing the last element of the circular buffer at the appropriate times. The statement ibuf (ibuf (N 1) ? 0 : ibuf) is a shorthand C way of incrementing ibuf such that it returns to 0 after reaching the end of the circular buffer array.

## Queues

Queues are also used in signal processing and event processing. Queues are used whenever data may arrive and depart at somewhat unpredictable times or when variable amounts of data may arrive. A queue is often referred to as an elastic buffer. One way to build a queue is with a linked list. This approach allows the queue to grow to an arbitrary size. But in many applications we are unwilling to pay the price of dynamically allocating memory. Another way to design the queue is to use an array to hold all the data. We used a circular buffer in Example 3.5 to manage interrupt-driven data; here we will develop a non-interrupt version. Programming Example 5.3 gives C code for a queue that is built from an array.

### Programming Example 4.3

### A buffer-based queue

The first step in designing the queue is to declare the array that we will use for the buffer:

#define Q_SIZE  32 /* your queue size  may vary */

#define Q_MAX (Q_SIZE-1) /* this is the maximum index value into the array */

int q[Q_SIZE]; /* the array for our queue */ We will use two variables to keep track of the state of the queue:

As our initialization code shows, we initialize them to the same position. As we add a value to the tail of the queue, we will increment tail. Similarly, when we remove a value from the head, we will increment head. When we reach the end of the array, we must wrap around these values—for example, when we add a value into the last element of q, the new value of tail becomes the 0th entry of the array.

void initialize_queue()    { head = 0;

tail = Q_MAX;

}

A useful function adds one to a value with wraparound:

Int      wrap(int i) { /* increment with wraparound for queue size */

```
return ((i+1) % Q_SIZE);

}
```

We need to check for two error conditions: removing from an empty queue and adding to a full queue. In the first case, we know the queue is empty if head wrap(tail). In the second case, we know the queue is full if incrementing tail will cause it to equal head. Testing for fullness, however, is a little harder since we have to worry about wraparound. Here is the code for adding an element to the tail of the queue, which is known as enqueueing:

```
enqueue(int val) {

/* check for a full queue */

if (wrap(wrap(tail) == head) error(ENQUEUE_ERROR);

/* update the tail */ tail = wrap(tail);

/* add val to the tail of the queue */ q[tail] = val;

}
```

And here is the code for removing an element from the head of the queue, known as dequeueing:

```
int     dequeue() {
int returnval; /* use this to remember the value that
you will return */
/* check for an empty queue */
if (head == wrap(tail)) error(DEQUEUE_ERROR);
/* remove from the head of the queue */ returnval = q[head];
/* update head */
head = wrap(head);
/* return the value */ return returnval;

}
```

## Models of Programs

Our fundamental model for programs is the control/data flow graph (CDFG). (We can also model hardware behavior with the CDFG.) As the name implies, the CDFG has constructs that model both data operations (arithmetic and other computations) and control operations (conditionals). Part of the power of the CDFG comes from its combination of control and data constructs. To understand the CDFG, we start with pure data descriptions and then extend the model to control.

### Data Flow Graphs

A data flowgraph is a model of a program with no conditionals. In a high-level programming language, a code segment with no conditionals—more precisely, with only one entry and exit point—is known as a basic block. Figure 5.2 shows a simple basic block. As the C code is executed, we would enter this basic block at the beginning and execute all the statements

### FIGURE4.2

A basic block in C.

w 5 a 1 b;

x15 a 2 c;

y 5 x1 1 d;

x25 a 1 c;

z 5 y 1 e;

FIGURE 4.3: The basic block in single-assignment form.

There are two assignments to the variable x—it appears twice on the left side of an assignment. We need to rewrite the code in single-assignment form, in which a variable appears only once on the left side. Since our specification is C code, we assume that the statements are executed sequentially, so that any use of a variable refers to its latest assigned value. In this case, x is not reused in this block (presumably it is used elsewhere), so we just have to eliminate the multiple assignment to x. The result is shown in Figure 5.3, where we have used the names x1 and x2 to distinguish the separate uses of x.

The single-assignment form is important because it allows us to identify a unique location in the code where each named location is computed. As an introduction to the data flow graph, we use two types of nodes in the graph—round nodes denote operators and square nodes represent values. The value nodes may be either inputs to the basic block, such as a and b, or variables assigned to within the block, such as w and x1. The data flow graph for our single-assignment code is shown in Figure 5.4. The single-assignment form means that the data flow graph is acyclic—if we assigned to x multiple times, then the second assignment would form a cycle in the graph including x and the operators used to compute x. Keeping the data flow graph acyclic is important in many types of analyses we want to do on the graph. (Of course,it is important to know whether the source code actually assigns to a variable multiple times, because some of those assignments may be mistakes. We consider the analysis of source code for proper use of assignments in Section 5.10.1). The data flow graph is generally drawn in the form shown in Figure 5.5. Here, the variables are not explicitly represented by nodes. Instead, the edges are labeled with the variables they represent.

### Control/Data Flow Graphs

A CDFG uses a data flow graph as an element, adding constructs to describe control. In a basic CDFG, we have two types of nodes: decision nodes and data flow nodes. A data flow node encapsulates a complete data flow graph to represent a basic block. We can use one type of decision node to describe all the types of control in a sequential program. (The jump/branch is, after all, the way we implement all those high-level control constructs.)

A bit of C code with control constructs and the CDFG constructed from it. The rectangular nodes in the graph represent the basic blocks. The basic blocks in the C code have been represented by function calls for simplicity. The diamond-shaped nodes represent the conditionals. The node's condition is given by the label, and the edges are labeled with the possible outcomes of evaluating the condition.

Building a CDFG for a while loop is straightforward, as shown in Figure 5.7. The while loop consists of both a test and a loop body, each of which we know how to represent in a CDFG. We can represent for loops by remembering that, in C, a for loop is defined in terms of a while loop. The following for loop

```
for (i = 0; i < N; i++) { loop_body();
}
```

is equivalent to

```
i = 0;
while (i < N) { loop_body(); i++;
}
```

For a complete CDFG model, we can use a data flow graph to model each data flow node. Thus, the CDFG is a hierarchical representation—a data flow CDFG can be expanded to reveal a complete data flow graph. An execution model for a CDFG is very much like the execution of the pro- gram it represents. The CDFG does not require explicit declaration of variables, but we assume that the implementation has sufficient memory for all the variables.

## Assembly, Linking, and Loading

Assembly and linking are the last steps in the compilation process— they turn a list of instructions into an image of the program's bits in memory. Loading actually puts the program in memory so that it can be executed. In this section, we survey the basic techniques required for assembly linking to help us understand the complete compilation and loading process. Highlights the role of assemblers and linkers in the compilation process.

This process is often hidden from us by compilation commands that do everything required to generate an executable program. As the figure shows, most compilers do not directly generate machine code, but instead create the instruction- level program in the form of human-readable assembly language. Gene- rating assembly language rather than binary instructions frees the compiler writer from details extraneous to the compilation process, which includes the instruction format as well as the exact addresses of instructions and data. The assembler's job is to translate symbolic assembly language statements into bit-level representations of instructions known as object code. The assembler takes care of instruction formats and does part of the job of translating labels into addresses. However, since the pro- gram may be built from many files, the final steps in determining the addresses of instructions and data are performed by the linker, which produces an executable binary file. That file may not necessarily be located in the CPU's memory, however, unless the linker happens to create the executable directly in RAM. The program that brings the program into memory for execution is called a loader.

The simplest form of the assembler assumes that the starting address of the assembly language program has been specified by the programmer. The addresses in such a program are known as absolute addresses. However, in many cases, particularly when we are creating an executable out of several component files, we do not want to specify the starting addresses for all the modules before assembly— if we did, we would have to determine before assembly not only the length of each program in memory but also the order in which they would be linked into the program.

Most assemblers therefore allow us to use relative addresses by specifying at the start of the file that the origin of the assembly language module is to be computed later. Addresses within the module are then computed relative to the start of the module. The linker is then responsible for translating relative addresses into addresses.

### *Assemblers*

When translating assembly code into object code, the assembler must translate opcodes and format the bits in each instruction, and translate labels into addresses. In this section, we review the translation of assembly language into binary.

Labels make the assembly process more complex, but they are the most important abstraction provided by the assembler. Labels let the programmer (a human programmer or a compiler generating assembly code) avoid worrying about the locations of instructions and data. Label processing requires making two passes through the assembly source code as follows:

- The first pass scans the code to determine the address of each label.
- The second pass assembles the instructions using the label values computed in the first pass.

As shown in Figure 5.9, the name of each symbol and its address is stored in a symbol table that is built during the first pass. The symbol table is built by scanning from the first instruction to the last. (For the moment, we assume that we know the address of the first instruction in the program; we consider the general case in Section 5.3.2.) During scanning, the current location in memory is kept in a program location counter (PLC). Despite the similarity in name to a pro- gram counter, the PLC is not used to execute the program, only to assign memory locations to labels. For example, the PLC always makes exactly one pass through the program, whereas the program counter makes many passes over code in a loop. Thus, at the start of the first pass, the PLC is set to the program's starting address and the assembler looks at the first line.

After examining the line, the assembler updates the PLC to the next location (since ARM instructions are four bytes long, the PLC would be incremented by four) and looks at the next instruction. If the instruction begins with a label, a new entry is made in the symbol table, which includes the label name and its value. The value of the label is equal to the current value of the PLC. At the end of the first pass, the assembler rewinds to the beginning of the assembly language file to make the second pass. During the second pass, when a label name is found, the label is looked up in the symbol table and its value substituted into the appropriate place in the instruction.

But how do we know the starting value of the PLC? The simplest case is absolute addressing. In this case, one of the first statements in the assembly language program is a pseudo-op that specifies the origin of the program, that is, the location of the first address in the program. A common name for this pseudo-op (e.g., the one used for the ARM) is the ORG statement

ORG 2000

which puts the start of the program at location 2000. This pseudo-op accomplishes this by setting the PLC's value to its argument's value, 2000 in this case. Assemblers generally allow a program to have many ORG statements in case instructions or data must be spread around various spots in memory.

*Example4.1*

*Generating a symbol table*

Let's use the following simple example of ARM assembly code:
ORG 100 label1 ADR r4,c LDR r0,[r4]
label2  ADR r4,d
LDR r1,[r4]
label3 SUB r0,r0,r1

The initial ORG statement tells us the starting address of the program. To begin, let's initialize the symbol table to an empty state and put the PLC at the initial ORG statement.

Assemblers allow labels to be added to the symbol table without occupying space in the program memory. A typical name of this pseudo-op is EQU for equate. For example, in the code

ADD r0,r1,r2 FOO  EQU 5

BAZ  SUB r3,r4,#FOO

The EQU pseudo-op adds a label named FOO with the value 5 to the symbol table. The value of the BAZ label is the same as if the EQU pseudo-op were not present, since EQU does not advance the PLC. The new label is used in the subsequent SUB instruction as the name for a constant. EQUs can be used to define symbolic values to help make the assembly code more structured. The ARM assembler supports one pseudo-op that is particular to the ARM instruction set. In other architectures, an address would be loaded into a register (e.g., for an indirect access) by reading it from a memory location. ARM does not have an instruction that can load an effective address, so the assembler supplies the ADR pseudo-op to create the address in the register. It does so by using ADD or SUB instructions to generate the address. The address to be loaded can be register relative, program relative, or numeric, but it must assemble to a single instruction. More complicated address calculations must be explicitly programmed. The assembler produces an object file that describes the instructions and data in binary format. A commonly used object file format, originally developed for Unix but now used in other environments as well, is known as COFF (common object file format). The object file must describe the instructions, data, and any addressing information and also usually carries along the symbol table for later use in debugging. Generating relative code rather than absolute code introduces some new challenges to the assembly language process. Rather than using an ORG statement to provide the starting address, the assembly code uses a pseudo-op to indicate that the code is in fact relocatable. (Relative code is the default for the ARM assembler.) Similarly, we must mark the output object file as being relative code. We can initialize the PLC to 0 to denote that addresses are relative to the start of the file.

However, when we generate code that makes use of those labels, we must be careful, since we do not yet know the actual value that must be put into the bits. We must instead generate relocatable code. We use extra bits in the object file format to mark the relevant fields as relocatable and then insert the label's relative value into the field. The linker must therefore modify the generated code-when it finds a field marked as relative, it uses the addresses that it has generated to replace the relative value with a correct, value for the address.To understand the details of turning relocatable code into executable code, we must understand the linking process described in the next section.

### Linking

Many assembly language programs are written as several smaller pieces rather than as a single large file. Breaking a large program into smaller files helps delineate A linker allows a program to be stitched together out of several smaller pieces. The linker operates on the object files created by the assembler and modifies the assembled code to make the necessary links between files. Some labels will be both defined and used in the same file. Other labels will be defined in a single file but used elsewhere as illustrated in Figure The place in the file where a label is defined is known as an entry point . The place in the file where the label is used is called an external reference. The main job of the loader is to resolve external references based on available entry points. As a result of the need to know how definitions and references connect, the assembler passes to the linker not only the object file but also the symbol table. Even if the entire symbol table is not kept for later debugging purposes, it must at least pass the entry points. External references are identified in the object code by their relative symbol identifiers. The linker proceeds in two phases. First, it determines the address of the start of each object file. The order in which object files are to be loaded is given by the user, either by specifying parameters when the loader is run or by creating a load map file that gives the order in which files are to be placed in memory. Given the order in which files are to be placed in memory and the length of each object file, it is easy to compute the starting address of each file. At the start of the second phase, the loader merges all symbol tables from the object files into a single, large table. It then edits the object files to change relative addresses into addresses. This is typically performed by having the assembler write extra bits into the object file to identify the instructions and fields that refer to labels. If a label cannot be found in the merged symbol table, it is undefined and an error message is sent to the user.

Controlling where code modules are loaded into memory is important in embedded systems. Some data structures and instructions, such as those used to manage interrupts, must be put at precise memory locations for them to work. In other cases, different types of memory may be installed at different address ranges. For example, if we have EPROM in some locations and DRAM in others, we want to make sure that locations to be written are put in the DRAM locations. Workstations and PCs provide dynamically linked libraries, and some embedded computing environments may provide them as well. Rather than link a separate copy of commonly used routines such as I/O to every executable program on the system, dynamically linked libraries allow them to be linked in at the start of program execution. A brief linking process is run just before execution of the program begins; the dynamic linker uses code libraries to link in the required routines. This not only saves storage space but also allows programs that use those libraries to be easily updated.

## Basic Compilation Techniques

It is useful to understand how a high-level language program is translated into instructions. Since implementing an embedded computing system often requires controlling the instruction sequences used to handle interrupts, placement of data and instructions in memory, and so forth, understanding how the compiler works can help you know when you cannot rely on the compiler. Next, because many applications are also performance sensitive, understanding how code is generated can help you meet your performance goals, either by writing high-level code that gets compiled into the instructions you want or by recognizing when you must write your own assembly code. Compilation combines translation and optimization. The high-level language program is translated into the lower-level form of instructions; optimizations try to generate better instruction sequences than would be possible if the brute force technique of independently translating source code statements were used. Optimization techniques focus on more of the program to ensure that compilation decisions that appear to be good for one statement are not unnecessarily problematic for other parts of the program.

The compilation process is summarized in Figure 5.11. Compilation begins with high-level language code such as C and generally produces assembly code. (Directly producing object code simply duplicates the functions of an assembler, Simplifying arithmetic expressions is one example of a machine-independent optimization. Not all compilers do such optimizations, and compilers can vary widely regarding which combinations of machine-independent optimizations they do perform. Instruction-level optimizations are aimed at generating code. They may work directly on real instructions or on a pseudo-instruction format that is later mapped onto the instructions of the target CPU. This level of optimization also helps modularize the compiler by allowing code generation to create simpler code that is later optimized. For example, consider the following array access code:

```
x[i] = c*x[i];
```

A simple code generator would generate the address for x[i] twice, once for each appearance in the statement. The later optimization phases can recognize this as an example of common expressions that need not be duplicated. While in this simple case it would be possible to create a code generator that never generated the redundant expression, taking into account every such optimization at code generation time is very difficult. We get better code and more reliable compilers by generating simple code first and then optimizing it.

### Statement Translation

In this section, we consider the basic job of translating the high-level language program with little or no optimization. Let's first consider how to translate an expression. A large amount of the code in a typical application consists of arithmetic and logical expressions. Understanding how to compile a single expression, as described in Example 4.2, is a good first step in understanding the entire compilation process.

*Example 4.2*

*Compiling an arithmetic expression*

In the following arithmetic expression,

a*b + 5*(c – d)

The variable is written in terms of program variables. In some machines we may be able to perform memory-to-memory arithmetic directly on the locations corresponding to those variables. However, in many machines, such as the ARM, we must first load the variables into registers. This requires choosing which registers receive not only the named variables but also intermediate results such as (c  d).

The code for the expression can be built by walking the data flow graph. The data flow graph for the expression appears on page 230.

The temporary variables for the intermediate values and final result have been named w, x, y, and z. To generate code, we walk from the tree's root (where z, the final result, is generated) by traversing the nodes in post order. During the walk, we generate instructions tocover the operation at every node. The path is presented below.

The nodes are numbered in the order in which code is generated. Since every node in the data flow graph corresponds to an operation that is directly supported by the instruction set, we simply generate an instruction at every node. Since we are making an arbitrary register assignment, we can use up the registers in order starting with r1. The resulting ARM code follows:

```
; operator 1 (+)
ADR r4,a          ; get address for a MOV r1,[r4]     ; load a
ADR r4,b          ; get address for b MOV r2,[r4]     ; load b
ADD r3,r1,r2      ; put w into r3
; operator 2 (−)
ADR r4,c          ; get address for c MOV r4,[r4]     ; load c
ADR r4,d          ; get address for d MOV r5,[r4]     ; load d
SUB r6,r4,r5      ; put x into r6
; operator 3 (*)
MUL r7,r6,#5      ; operator 3, puts y into r7
; operator 4 (+)
ADD r8,r7,r3      ; operator 4, puts z into r8
```

One obvious optimization is to reuse a register whose value is no longer needed. In the case of the intermediate values w, x, and y, we know that they cannot be used after the end of the expression (e.g., in another expression) since they have no name in the C program. However, the final result z may in fact be used in a C assignment and the value reused later in the program.

### Procedures

Another major code generation problem is the creation of procedures. Generating code for procedures is relatively straightforward once we know the procedure link- age appropriate for the CPU. At the procedure definition, we generate the code to handle the procedure call and return. At each call of the procedure, we set up the procedure parameters and make the call.

The CPU's subroutine call mechanism is usually not sufficient to directly support procedures in modern programming languages. We introduced the procedure stack and procedure linkages in Section 2.2.3. The linkage mechanism provides a way for the program to pass parameters into the program and for the procedure to return a value. It also provides help in restoring the values of registers that the procedure has modified. All procedures in a given programming language use the same linkage mechanism (although different languages may use different linkages). The mechanism can also be used to call handwritten assembly language routines from compiled code.

Procedure stacks are typically built to grow down from high addresses. A stack pointer (sp) defines the end of the current frame, while a frame pointer (fp) defines the end of the last frame. (The fp is technically necessary only if the stack frame can be grown by the procedure during execution.) The procedure can refer

The ARM Procedure Call Standard (APCS) is a good illustration of a typi- cal procedure linkage mechanism. Although the stack frames are in main memory, understanding how registers are used is key to understanding the mechanism, as explained below.

- $r0$  $r3$ are used to pass parameters into the procedure. $r0$ is also used  to hold the return value. If more than four parameters are required, they are  put on the  stack frame.
- $r4$  $r7$ hold register variables.
- $r11$ is the frame pointer and $r13$ is the stack  pointer.
- $r10$ holds the limiting address  on stack  size, which is used  to check  for stack overflows.

  Other registers have additional uses in the  protocol.

## Data Structures

The compiler must also translate references to data structures into references to raw memories. In general, this requires address computations. Some of these computations can be done at compile time while others must be done at run time. Arrays are interesting because the address of an array element must in general be computed at run time, since the array index may change. Let us first consider one-dimensional arrays:

$$a[i]$$

The layout of the array in memory is shown in Figure 5.13. The zeroth element is stored as the first element of the array, the first element directly below, and  so on.

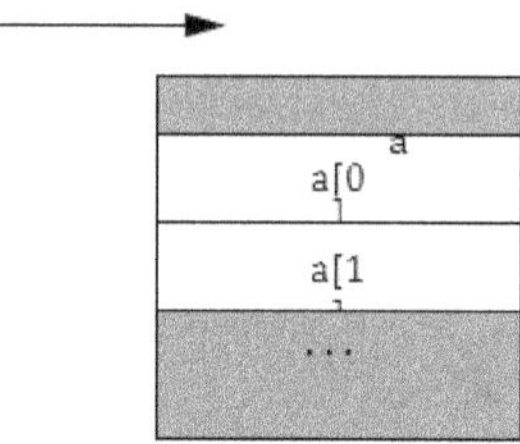



Figure 4.13: Layout of a one-dimensional array  in  memory

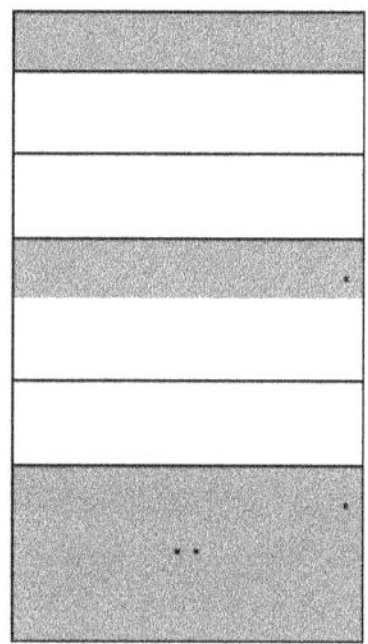

Figure 4.14: Memory  layout  for  two-dimensional arrays

We can create a pointer for the array that points to the array's head, namely, a[0]. If we call that pointer aptr for convenience, then we can rewrite the reading of a[i] as

*(aptr + i)

Two-dimensional arrays are more challenging. There are multiple possible ways to lay out a two-dimensional array in memory, as shown in Figure 5.14. In this form, which is known as row major , the inner variable of the array ( j in a[i, j]) varies most quickly. (Fortran uses a different organization known as column major.) Two- dimensional arrays also require more sophisticated addressing—in particular, we must know  the size of the array. Let us consider the row-major  form. If the a[] array is of size N M , then we can turn the two-dimensional array access into a one- dimensional array access. Thus,

a[i,j] becomes a[i*M + j]

where the maximum value for j is M 1.

A C struct is easier to address. As shown in Figure 5.15, a structure is implemented as a contiguous block of memory. Fields in the structure can be accessed using constant offsets to the base address of the structure. In this example, if field1 is four bytes long, then field2 can be accessed as

*(aptr + 4)

This addition can usually be done at compile time, requiring only the indirection itself to fetch the memory location during execution.

## Program Optimization

Now that we understand something about how programs are created,we can start to understand how to optimize programs. If we want to write programs in a high- level language, then we need to understand how to optimize them without rewriting them in assembly language. This first requires creating the proper source code that causes the compiler to do what we want. Hopefully, the compiler can optimize our program by recognizing features of the code and taking the proper action.

### *Expression Simplification*

Expression simplification is a useful area for machine-independent transforma- tions. We can use the laws of algebra to simplify expressions. Consider the following expression:

a*b + a*c

We can use the distributive law to rewrite the expression as a*(b + c). Since the new expression has only two operations rather than three for the original form, it is almost certainly cheaper, because it is both faster and smaller. Such transformations make some broad assumptions about the relative cost of operations. In some cases, simple generalizations about the cost of operations may be misleading. For example, a CPU with a multiply-and-accumulate instruction may be able to do a multiply and addition as cheaply as it can do an addition. However, such situations can often be taken care of in code generation. We can also use the laws of arithmetic to further simplify expressions on constants. Consider the following C statement:

    for (i = 0; i < 8 + 1; i++)
    We can simplify 8 1 to 9 at compile time—there is no need to perform that arithmetic while the program is executing. Why would a program ever contain expressions that evaluate to constants? Using named constants rather than numbers is good programming practice and often leads to constant expression. The original form of the for statement could have been

for (i = 0; i < NOPS + 1; i++)

where, for example, the added 1 takes care of a trailing null character.

### Dead Code Elimination

Code that will never be executed can be safely removed from the program. The general problem of identifying code that will never be executed is difficult, but there are some important special cases where it can be done. Programmers will intentionally introduce dead code in certain situations. Consider this C code fragment:

```
#define DEBUG 0

...

if (DEBUG) print_debug_stuff();
```

In the above case, the print_debug_stuff( ) function is never executed, but the code allows the programmer to override the preprocessor variable definition (per- haps with a compile-time flag) to enable the debugging code. This case is easy to analyze because the condition is the constant 0, which C uses for the false condition. Since there is no else clause in the if statement, the compiler can totally eliminate the if statement, rewriting the CDFG to provide a direct edge between the statements before and after the if.

### Procedure Inlining

Another machine-independent transformation that requires a little more evalua- tion is procedure inlining. An inlined procedure does not have a separate proce- dure body and procedure linkage; rather, the body of the procedure is substituted in place for the procedure calining in C.

```
                   int foo(a,b,c) { return a 1 b 2 c; }
Function definition

z 5 foo(w,x,y); Function call z 5 w 1 x 2 y;
```

### Inlining result

The C++ programming language provides an inline construct that tells the compiler to generate inline code for a function. In this case, an inlined procedure is generated in expanded form whenever possible. However, inlining is not always the best thing to do. Although it does eliminate the procedure linkage instructions, when a cache is present, having multiple copies of the function body may actually slow down the fetches of these instructions. Inlining also increases code size, and memory may be precious.

### *Loop Transformations*

Loops are important program structures—although they are compactly described in the source code, they often use a large fraction of the computation time. Many techniques have been designed to optimize loops.

A simple but useful transformation is known as loop unrolling , which is illustrated in Example 5.4. Loop unrolling is important because it helps expose parallelism that can be used by later stages of the compiler.

*Example 4.4*
Loop unrolling

A simple loop in C follows:

```
for (i = 0; i < N; i++) {

a[i] = b[i]*c[i];

}
```

This loop is executed a fixed number of times, namely, N. A straightforward implementation of the loop would create and initialize the loop variable i , update its value on every iteration, and test it to see whether to exit the loop. However, since the loop is executed a fixed number of times, we can generate more direct code.

If we let $N4$, then we can substitute the above C code for the following loop:

```
a[0] = b[0]*c[0];

a[1] = b[1]*c[1];
```

fig

Example 4.5

### *Register allocation*

To keep the example small, we assume that we can use only four of the ARM's registers. In fact, such a restriction is not unthinkable—programming conventions can reserve certain registers for special purposes and significantly reduce the number of general-purpose registers available. Consider the following C code:

```
w = a + b;  /* statement 1 */ x  = c +  w;  /* statement 2
*/ y = c + d;  /* statement 3  */
```

A naive register allocation, assigning each variable to a separate register, would require seven registers for the seven variables in the above code. However, we can do much better by reusing a register once the value stored in the register is no longer needed. To understand how to do this, we can draw a lifetime graph that shows the statements on which each statement is used. Appearing below is a lifetime graph in which the x -axis is the statement number in the C code and the y -axis shows the variables.

A horizontal line stretches from the first statement where the variable is used to the last use of the variable; a variable is said to be live during this interval. At each statement, we can determine every variable currently in use. The maximum number of variables in use at any statement determines the maximum number of registers required. In this case, statement two requires three registers: c , w , and x . This fits within the four registers limitation. By reusing registers once their current values are no longer needed, we can write code that requires no more than four registers. Appearing below is one register assignment.

The ARM assembly code that uses the above register assignment follows:

```
            LDR r0,[p_a] ; load a into  r0 using pointer
to  a (p_a) LDR r1,[p_b]    ; load b into  r1
            ADD r3,r0,r1            ; compute a + w = a  b
            STR r3,[p_w] LDR       ; + b load  c into
            r2,[p_c] ADD           ; compute c +          r2
                                   ;                w,        reusing r0
            r0,r2,r3                                                 for  x
            STR r0,[p_x]           ; x = c + w
            LDR r0,[p_d]           ; load  d into         r0
            ADD r3,r2,r0           ; compute c +          d, reusing r3
                                                                     for  y
            STR r3,[p_y]           ; y = c + d
```

*Example 4.6*

### *Operator scheduling for register allocation*

Here is sample C code fragment:

w = a + b; /* statement 1 */ x  = c + d; /* statement 2

*/ y = x + e; /* statement 3 */ z = a – b; /* statement  4 */

Since w is needed until the last statement, we need five registers at statement 3, even though only three registers are needed for the statement at line 3. If we swap statements 3 and 4 (renumbering them 39 and 49), we reduce our requirements to three registers. The modified C code follows:

w = a + b; /* statement 1 */

z = a – b; /* statement 29 */ x = c + d; /* statement  39

*/ y = x + e; /* statement 49 */

Compare the ARM assembly code for the two code  fragments.  We have  written both assuming that we have only four free registers. In the before version, we do not have to write out any values, but we must read a and b twice. The after version allows us to retain all values in registers as long as we need them.

| Before version | After version |
|---|---|
| LDR r0,a | LDR r0,a |
| LDR r1,b | LDR r1,b |
| ADD r2,r0,r1 | ADD r2,r1,r0 |
| STR r2,w; w = a + b | STR r2,w; |
| | |
| w = a + b LDRr r0,c | SUB |
| | |
| r2,r0,r1 | |
| | |
| LDR r1,d | STR r2,z ; z = a – b |
| ADD r2,r0,r1 | LDR r0,c |
| STR r2,x ; x = c + d | LDR r1,d |
| LDR r1,e | ADD r2,r1,r0 |
| ADD r0,r1,r2 | STR r2,x ; |
| | |
| x = c + d STR r0,y ; y = x + e LDR r1,e | |
| | |
| LDR r0,a ; reload  a | ADD r0,r1,r2 |
| LDR r1,b; reload b | STR r0,y ; |
| | |
| y = x+ e SUB r2,r1,r0 | |
| | |
| STR r2,z ; z = a – b | |

Register allocation by changing the order in which operations are performed, thereby changing the lifetimes of the variables.

We can keep track of CPU resources during instruction scheduling using a reservation table [Kog81] As illustrated in Figure 5.19, rows in the table represent instruction execution time slots and columns represent resources that must be scheduled. Before scheduling an instruction to be executed at a particular time, we check the reservation table to determine whether all resources needed by the instruction are available at that time. Upon scheduling the instruction, we update the table to note all resources used by that instruction. Various algorithms can be used for the scheduling itself, depending on the types of resources and instructions involved, but the reservation table provides a good summary of the state of an instruction scheduling problem in progress.

We can also schedule instructions to maximize performance. As we know from Section 3.5, when an instruction that takes more cycles than normal to finish is in the pipeline, pipeline bubbles appear that reduce performance. Software pipelining is a technique for reordering instructions across several loop iterations to reduce pipeline bubbles. Some instructions take several cycles to complete; if the value produced by one of these instructions is needed by other instructions in the loop iteration, then they must wait for that value to be produced. Rather than pad the loop with no-ops, we can start instructions from the next iteration. The loop body then contains instructions that manipulate values from several different loop iterations— some of the instructions are working on the early part of iteration n 1, others are working on iteration n, and still others are finishing iteration n 1.

### *Instruction Selection*

Selecting the instructions to use to implement each operation is not trivial. There may be several different instructions that can be used to accomplish the same goal, but they may have different execution times. Moreover, using one instruction for one part of the program may affect the instructions that can be used in adjacent code. Although we cannot discuss all the problems and methods for code generation here, a little bit of knowledge helps us envision what the compiler is doing. One useful technique for generating code is template matching, illustrated in Figure 5.20. We have a DAG that represents the expression for which we want to generate code. In order to be able to match up instructions and operations, we represent instructions using the same DAG representation. We shaded the instruction template nodes to distinguish them from code nodes. Each node has a cost, which may be simply the execution time of the instruction or may include factors for size, power consumption, and so on. In this case, we have shown that each instruction takes the same amount of time, and thus all have a cost of 1. Our goal is to cover all nodes in the code DAG with instruction DAGs—until we have covered the code DAG we have not generated code for all the operations in the expression.

### Understanding and Using Your Compiler

Clearly, the compiler can vastly transform your program during the creation of assembly language. But compilers are also substantially different in terms of the optimizations they perform. Understanding your compiler can help you get the best code out of it.

Studying the assembly language output of the compiler is a good way to learn about what the compiler does. Some compilers will annotate sections of code to help you make the correspondence between the source and assembler output. Starting with small examples that exercise only a few types of statements will help. You can experiment with different optimization levels (the -O flag on most C compilers). You can also try writing the same algorithm in several ways to see how the compiler's output changes.

If you cannot get your compiler to generate the code you want, you may need to write your own assembly language. You can do this by writing it from scratch or modifying the output of the compiler. If you write your own assembly code, you must ensure that it conforms to all compiler conventions, such as procedure call linkage. If you modify the compiler output, you should be sure that you have the algorithm right before you start writing code so that you don't have to repeatedly edit the compiler's assembly language output. You also need to clearly document the fact that the high- level language source is, in fact, not the code used in the system.

### Interpreters and JIT Compilers

Programs are not always compiled and then separately executed. In some cases, it may make sense to translate the program into instructions during execution. Two well-known techniques for on-the-fly translation are interpretation and just-in-time (JIT ) compilation. The trade-offs for both techniques are similar. Interpretation or JIT compilation adds overhead—both time and memory—to execution. However, that overhead may be more than made up for in some circum- stances. For example, if only parts of the program are executed over some period of time, interpretation or JIT compilation may save memory, even taking overhead into account. Interpretation and JIT compilation also provide added security when programs arrive over the network.

An interpreter translates program statements one at a time. The program may be expressed in a high-level language, with Forth being a prime example of an embedded language that is interpreted. An interpreter may also interpret instructions in some abstract machine language. As illustrated in Figure 5.21, the interpreter sits between the program and the machine. It translates one statement of the program at a time. The interpreter may or may not generate an explicit piece of code to represent the statement. Because the interpreter translates only a very small piece of the program at any given time, a small amount of memory is used to hold inter- mediate representations of the program. In many cases, a Forth program plus the Forth interpreter are smaller than the equivalent native machine code.

## Program-level Performance Analysis

Because embedded systems must perform functions in real time, we often need to know how fast a program runs. The techniques we use to analyze program execution time are also helpful in analyzing properties such as power consumption. In this we might hope that the execution time of programs could be precisely determined, this is in fact difficult to do in practice:

- The execution time of a program often varies with the input data values because those values select different execution paths in the program. For example, loops may be executed a varying number of times, and different branches may execute blocks of varying complexity.
- The cache has a major effect on program performance, and once again, the cache's behavior depends in part on the data values input to the program.
- Execution times may vary even at the instruction level. Floating-point operations are the most sensitive to data values, but the normal integer execution pipeline can also introduce data-dependent variations. In general, the execution time of an instruction in a pipeline depends not only on that instruction but on the instructions around it in the pipeline.
- We can measure program performance in several ways:
- Some microprocessor manufacturers supply simulators for their CPUs: The simulator runs on a workstation or PC, takes as input an executable for the microprocessor along with input data, and simulates the execution of that pro-gram. Some of these simulators go beyond functional simulation to measure the execution time of the program. Simulation is clearly slower than executing the program on the actual microprocessor, but it also provides much greater visibility during execution. Be careful—some microprocessor performance simulators are not 100% accurate, and simulation of I/O-intensive code may be difficult.
- A timer connected to the microprocessor bus can be used to measure performance of executing sections of code. The code to be measured would reset and start the timer at its start and stop the timer at the end of execution. The length of the program

that can be measured is limited by the accuracy of the timer.

- A logic analyzer can be connected to the microprocessor bus to measure the start and stop times of a code segment. This technique relies on the code being able to produce identifiable events on the bus to identify the start and stop of execution. The length of code that can be measured is limited by the size of the logic analyzer's buffer.

- ***Average-case execution time*** This is the typical execution time we would expect for typical data. Clearly, the first challenge is defining typical inputs.

- ***Worst-case execution time*** The longest time that the program can spend on any input sequence is clearly important for systems that must meet dead- lines. In some cases, the input set that causes the worst-case execution time is obvious, but in many cases it is not.

- ***Best-case execution time:*** This measure can be important in multirate real-time systems, as seen in Chapter 6.

First, we look at the fundamentals of program performance in more detail. We then consider trace-driven performance based on executing the program and observing its behavior.

### *Elements of Program Performance*

The key to evaluating execution time is breaking the performance problem into parts. Program execution time [Sha89] can be seen as

execution time        program path    instruction timing

Not all instructions take the same amount of time. Although RISC architectures tend to provide uniform instruction execution times in order to keep the CPU's pipeline full, even many RISC architectures take different amounts of time to execute certain instructions. Multiple load-store instructions are examples of longer- executing instructions in the ARM architecture. Floating- point instructions show especially wide variations in execution time—while basic multiply and add operations are fast, some transcendental functions can take thousands of cycles to execute.

- Execution times of instructions are not independent. The execution time of one instruction depends on the instructions around it. For example, many CPUs use register bypassing to speed up instruction sequences when the result of one instruction is used in the next instruction.

- As a result, the execution time of an instruction may depend on whether its destination register is used as a source for the next operation (or vice versa).

- The execution time of an instruction may depend on operand values. This is clearly true of floating-point instructions in which a different number of iterations may be required to calculate the result. Other specialized instructions can, for example, perform a data-dependent number of integer operations.

We can handle the first two problems more easily than the third. We can look up instruction execution time in a table; the table will be indexed by opcode and possibly by other parameter values such as the registers used. To handle interdependent execution times, we can add columns to the table to consider the effects of nearby instructions. Since these effects are generally limited by the size of the CPU pipeline, we know that we need to consider a relatively small window of instructions to handle such effects. Handling variations due to operand values is difficult to do without actually executing the program using a variety of data values, given the large number of factors that can affect value-dependent instruction timing. Luckily, these effects are often small. Even in floating-point programs, most of the operations are typically additions and multiplications whose execution times have small variances. Thus far we have not considered the effect of the cache. Because the access time for main memory can be 10–100 times larger than the cache access time, caching can have huge effects on instruction execution time by changing both the instruction and data access times. Caching performance inherently depends on the program's execution path since the cache's contents depend on the history of accesses.

### Measurement-Driven Performance Analysis

The most direct way to determine the execution time of a program is by measuring it. This approach is appealing, but it does have some drawbacks. First, in order to cause the program to execute its worst-case execution path, we have to provide the proper inputs to it. Determining the set of inputs that will guarantee the worst- case execution path is infeasible. Furthermore, in order to measure the program's performance on a particular type of CPU, we need the CPU or its simulator. Despite these drawbacks, measurement is the most commonly used way to determine the execution time of embedded software. Worst-case execution time analysis algorithms have been used successfully in some areas, such as flight control software, but many system design projects determine the execution time of their programs by measurement. The other problem with input data is the software scaffolding that we may need to feed data into the program and get data out. When we are designing a large system, it may be difficult to extract out part of the software and test it independently of the other parts of the system. We may need to add new testing modules to the system software to help us introduce testing values and to observe testing outputs.

We can measure program performance either directly on the hardware or by using a simulator. Each method has its advantages and disadvantages.

Physical measurement requires some sort of hardware instrumentation. The most direct method of measuring the performance of a program would be to watch the program counter's value: start a timer when the PC reaches the program's start, stop the timer when it reaches the program's end. Unfortunately, it generally isn't possible to directly observe the program counter. However, it is possible in many cases to

modify the program so that it starts a timer at the beginning of execution and stops the timer at the end. While this doesn't give us direct information about the program trace, it does give us execution time. If we have several timers available, we can use them to measure the execution time of different parts of the program. A logic analyzer or an oscilloscope can be used to watch for signals that mark various points in the execution of the program. However, because logic analyzers have a limited amount of memory, this approach doesn't work well for programs with extremely long execution times.

Some CPUs have hardware facilities for automatically generating trace information. For example, the Pentium family microprocessors generate a special bus cycle,a branch trace message, that shows the source and/or destination address of a branch [Col97]. If we record only traces, we can reconstruct the instructions executed within the basic blocks while greatly reducing the amount of memory required to hold the trace.

The alternative to physical measurement of execution time is simulation. A CPU simulator is a program that takes as input a memory image for a CPU and performs the operations on that memory image that the actual CPU would perform, leaving

To start the simulation process, we compile our test program using a special compiler:

```
% arm-linux-gcc firtest.c
```

This gives us an executable program (by default, a.out) that we use to simulate our program:

```
% arm-outorder a.out
```

SimpleScalar produces a large output file with a great deal of information about the program's execution. Since this is a simple example, the most useful piece of data is the total number of simulated clock cycles required to execute the program:

```
sim_cycle 25854 # total simulation time in
```

cycles

To make sure that we can ignore the effects of program overhead, we will execute the FIR filter for several different values of N and compare. This run used N 100; when we also run N 1,000 and N 10,000, we get these results:

| Total | simulation time |
|-------|-----------------|
| 25854 | 259 |
| 15575 | 156 |
| 14518 | 145 |
| 0000 | 40 |

Because the FIR filter is so simple and ran in so few cycles, we had to execute it a number of times to wash out all the other overhead of program execution. However, the time for 1,000 and 10,000 filter executions are within 10% of each other, so those values are reasonably close to the actual execution time of the FIR filter itself.

## Software Performance Optimization

In this section we will look at several techniques for optimizing software perfor- mance.

### *Loop Optimizations*

Loops are important targets for optimization because programs with loops tend to spend a lot of time executing those loops. There are three important techniques in optimizing loops: code motion, induction variable elimination, and strength reduction. Code motion lets us move unnecessary code out of a loop. If a computation's result does not depend on operations performed in the loop body,then we can safely move it out of the loop. Code motion opportunities can arise because programmers may find some computations clearer and more concise when put in the loop body, even though they are not strictly dependent on the loop iterations. A simple example of code motion is also common. Consider the following loop:

```
for (i = 0; i < N*M; i++)

{

z[i] = a[i] + b[i];

}
```

The code motion opportunity becomes more obvious when we draw the loop's CDFG as shown in Figure 5.23. The loop bound computation is performed on every iteration during the loop  test, even  though  the  result  never  changes. We can  avoid N    M  1 unnecessary executions of this statement by moving it before the loop, as shown  in  the  figure.

An induction variable is a variable whose value is derived from the loop iteration  variable's value. The  compiler  often  introduces  induction  variables  to  help  it  implement  the  loop. Properly  transformed,  we  may  be  able  to  eliminate  some  variables  and  apply  strength reduction to others. A nested  loop  is  a  good  example  of  the   use   of  induction  variables. Here is  a simple  nested  loop:

```
for  (i  =  0;  i  <  N;  i++)

for  (j  =  0;  j  <  M;  j++)

z[i][j]  = b[i][j];
```

The compiler uses induction variables to help it address the arrays. Let us rewrite the loop in  C  using  induction  variables  and  pointers.  (Later,  we  use  a common induction variable for the  two  arrays,  even  though  the  compiler  would probably introduce separate induction variables and  then  merge   them.)

```
for  (i  =  0;  i  <  N;  i++)

for  (j  =  0;  j  <  M;  j++)

{

zbinduct = i*M  + j;

*(zptr  +  zbinduct)   =  *(bptr  +  zbinduct);

}
```

In the above code, zptr and bptr are pointers to  the  heads  of  the  z  and  b arrays and zbinduct is the shared induction variable. However, we do not need to compute zbinduct afresh each time. Since we  are  stepping  through  the  arrays  sequentially, we can  simply add  the  update  value to the  induction variable:

```
zbinduct = 0;

for  (i  =  0;  i  <  N;  i++)  { for  (j  =  0;  j  <  M;  j++)  {

*(zptr + zbinduct) = *(bptr + zbinduct); zbinduct++;

}

}
```

This is a form of strength reduction since we have eliminated the multiplication from  the induction variable   computation. Strength reduction helps us reduce  the  cost  of  a  loop iteration. Consider  the  following assignment:

$$y = x * 2;$$

In integer arithmetic, we can use a left shift rather than a multiplication  by 2  (as  long as we  properly  keep  track  of  overflows). If  the  shift  is  faster than the multiply, we  probably want  to  perform  the  substitution.  This optimization can often  be  used  with  induction variables  because  loops  are  often indexed with simple expressions. Strength  reduction  can often be performed with  simple substitution rules since there are  relatively  few  interactions between  the  possible  substitutions.

### Cache Optimizations

A loop nest is a  set  of loops,  one  inside  the  other.  Loop  nests  occur when we process arrays. A large body of techniques has been  developed for optimizing loop nests. Rewriting a loop nest changes the order in which array elements are accessed. This can   expose new parallelism opportunities that can  be exploited by later  stages of the compiler, and it can  also improve cache performance. In this  section  we concentrate on the  analysis of loop  nests for cache performance.

### Example 5.10

### Data realignment and array padding

Assume we want to optimize the cache  behavior of the following  code:

for (j = 0; j < M; j++)

for (i = 0; i < N; i++)

a[j][i] = b[j][i] * c;

Let us also assume that the a and b arrays are sized with M at 265 and  N  at 4 and a 256-line, four-way set-associative cache with four words per line. Even though this code does  not reuse any data elements,  cache  conflicts can  cause  serious  performance problems because they interfere with spatial  reuse  at the cache  line level.

Assume  that the starting location for a[] is 1024  and  the starting location for  b[] is 4099. Although a[0][0] and b[0][0] do not map to the same word in the cache, they do map  to the same block. As a result, we see the following scenario  in execution:

- The access to a[0][0] brings  in  the  first four words of  a[].

- The access to $b[0][0]$ replaces $a[0][0]$ through $a[0][3]$ with $b[0][3]$ and the contents of the three locations before $b[]$.

- When $a[0][1]$ is accessed, the same cache line is again replaced with the first four elements of $a[]$.

Once the a[0][1] access brings that line into the cache, it remains there for the a[0][2] and a[0][3] accesses since the b[] accesses are now on the next line. However, the scenario repeats itself at a[1][0] and every four iterations of the cache.

One way to eliminate the cache conflicts is to move one of the arrays. We do not have to move it far. If we move b's start to 4100, we eliminate the cache conflicts.

However, that fix won't work in more complex situations. Moving one array may only introduce cache conflicts with another array. In such cases, we can use another technique called padding. If we extend each of the rows of the arrays to have four elements rather than three, with the padding word placed at the beginning of the row, we eliminate the cache conflicts. In this case, b[0][0] is located at 4100 by the padding. Although padding wastes memory, it substantially improves memory performance. In complex situations with multiple arrays and sophisticated access patterns, we have to use a combination of techniques—relocating arrays and padding them—to be able to minimize cache conflicts.

### *Performance Optimization Strategies*

Let's look more generally at how to improve program execution time. First, make sure that the code really needs to be accelerated. If you are dealing with a large program, the part of the program using the most time may not be obvious. Profiling the program will help you find hot spots. A profiler does not measure execution time-=instead, it counts the number of times that procedures or basic blocks in the program

are executed. There are two major ways to profile a program: We can modify the executable program by adding instructions that increment a location every time the program passes that point in the program; or we can sample the program counter during execution and keep track of the distribution of PC values. Profiling adds relatively little overhead to the program and it gives us some useful information about where the program spends most of its time.

You may be able to redesign your algorithm to improve efficiency. Examining asymptotic performance is often a good guide to efficiency. Doing fewer operations is usually the key to performance. In a few cases, however, brute force may provide a better implementation. A seemingly simple high-level language statement may in fact hide a very long sequence of operations that slows down the algorithm.Using dynamically allocated memory is one example, since managing the heap takes time but is hidden from the programmer. For example, a sophisticated algorithm that uses dynamic storage may be slower in practice than an algorithm that performs more operations on statically allocated memory. Finally, you can look at the implementation of the program itself. A few hints on program implementation are summarized below.

- Try to use registers efficiently. Group accesses to a value together so that the value can be brought into a register and kept there.

- Make use of page mode accesses in the memory system whenever possible. Page mode reads and writes eliminate one step in the memory access. You can increase use of page mode by rearranging your variables so that more can be referenced contiguously.

- Analyze cache behavior to find major cache conflicts. Restructure the code to eliminate as many of these as you can as follows:

  For instruction conflicts, if the offending code segment is small, try to rewrite the segment to make it as small as possible so that it better fits into the cache. Writing in assembly language may be necessary. For conflicts across larger spans of code, try moving the instructions or padding with NOPs.

  For scalar data conflicts, move the data values to different locations to reduce conflicts.

- For array data conflicts, consider either moving the arrays or changing your array access patterns to reduce conflicts.

**Program-Level Energy and Power Analysis and Optimization**

Power consumption is a particularly important design metric for battery- powered systems because the battery has a very limited lifetime. However, power consumption is increasingly important in systems that run off the power grid. Fast chips run hot, and controlling power consumption is an important element of increasing reliability and reducing system cost. How much control do we have over power consumption? Ultimately, we must consume the energy required to perform necessary computations. However, there are opportunities for saving power. Examples appear below.

- We may be able to replace the algorithms with others that do things in clever ways that consume less power.

- Memory accesses are a major component of power consumption in many applications.By optimizing memory accesses we may be able to significantly reduce power.

- We may be able to turn off parts of the system—such as subsystems of the CPU, chips in the system, and so on—when we do not need them in order to save power.

The first step in optimizing a program's energy consumption is knowing how much energy the program consumes. It is possible to measure power consumption for an instruction or a small code fragment [Tiw94]. The technique, illustrated in Figure 5.24, executes the code under test over and over in a loop. By measuring the current flowing into the CPU, we are measuring the power consumption of the complete loop, including both the body and other code. By separately measuring the power consumption of a loop with no body (making sure, of course, that the compiler hasn't optimized away the empty loop), we can calculate the power con- sumption of the loop body code as the difference between the full loop and the bare loop energy cost of an instruction. Several factors contribute to the energy consumption of the program.

- Energy consumption varies somewhat from instruction to instruction.
- The sequence of instructions has some influence.
- Th opcode and the locations of the operands also matter.
- A few optimizations mentioned previously for performance are also often useful for improving energy consumption:
- Try to use registers efficiently. Group accesses to a value together so that the value can be brought into a register and kept there.
- Analyze cache behavior to find major cache conflicts. Restructure the code to eliminate as many of these as you can:

  For instruction conflicts, if the offending code segment is small, try to rewrite the segment to make it as small as possible so that it better fits into the cache. Writing in assembly language may be necessary. For conflicts across larger spans of code, try moving the instructions or padding with NOPs.

  For scalar data conflicts, move the data values to different locations to reduce conflicts. For array data conflicts, consider either moving the arrays or changing your array access patterns to reduce conflicts.

- Make use of page mode accesses in the memory system whenever possible. Page mode reads and writes eliminate one step in the memory access, saving a considerable amount of power.

## Analysis and Optimization of Program Size

The memory footprint of a program is determined by the size of its data and instructions. Both must be considered to minimize program size. Data provide an excellent opportunity for minimizing size because the data are most highly dependent on programming style. Because inefficient programs often keep several copies of data, identifying and eliminating duplications can lead to significant memory savings usually with little performance penalty. Buffers should be sized carefully—rather than defining a data array to a large size that the pro- gram will never attain, determine the actual maximum amount of data held in the buffer and allocate the array accordingly. Data can sometimes be packed, such as by storing several flags in a single word and extracting them by using bit-level operations.

A very low-level technique for minimizing data is to reuse values. For instance, if several constants happen to have the same value, they can be mapped to the same location. Data buffers can often be reused at several different points in the program. This technique must be used with extreme caution, however, since subsequent versions of the program may not use the same values for the constants. A more generally applicable technique is to generate data on the fly rather than store it. Of course, the code required to generate the data takes up space in the program, but when complex data structures are involved there may be some net space savings from using code to generate data. Minimizing the size of the instruction text of a program requires a mix of high-level program transformations and careful instruction selection. Encapsulating functions in subroutines can reduce program size when done carefully. Because sub-routines have overhead for parameter passing that is not obvious from the high-level language code, there is a minimum-size function body for which a subroutine makes sense. Architectures that have variable-size instruction lengths are particularly good candidates for careful coding to minimize program size, which may require assembly language coding of key program segments. There may also be cases in which one or a sequence of instructions is much smaller than alternative implementations-for example, a multiply-accumulate instruction may be both smaller and faster than separate arithmetic operations.

## Program Validation and Testing

Complex systems need testing to ensure that they work as they are intended. But bugs can be subtle, particularly in embedded systems, where specialized hardware and real-time responsiveness make programming more challenging. Fortunately, there are many available techniques for software testing that can help us generate a comprehensive set of tests to ensure that our system works properly. We examine the role of validation in the overall design methodology in Section 9.5. In this section, we concentrate on nuts-and-bolts techniques for creating a good set of tests for a given program.

The first question we must ask ourselves is how much testing is enough. Clearly, we cannot test the program for every possible combination of inputs. Because we cannot implement an infinite number of tests, we naturally ask ourselves what a reasonable standard of thoroughness is. One of the major contributions of soft- ware testing is to provide us with standards of thoroughness that make sense. Following these standards does not guarantee that we will find all bugs. But by breaking the testing problem into subproblems and analyzing each subproblem. The two major types of testing strategies:

***Black-box*** methods generate tests without looking at the internal structure of the program.

***Clear-box*** (also known as ***white-box***) methods generate tests based on the program structure.

In this section we cover both types of tests, which complement each other by exercising programs in very different ways.

### Clear-Box Testing

The control/data flow graph extracted from a program's source code is an important tool in developing clear-box tests for the program. To adequately test the program, we must exercise both its control and data operations. In order to execute and evaluate these tests, we must be able to control variables in the program and observe the results of computations, much as in manufacturing testing. In general, we may need to modify the program to make it more testable. By adding new inputs and outputs, we can usually substantially reduce the effort required to find and execute the test. Example 5.11 illustrates the importance of observability and controllability in software testing. No matter what we are testing, we must accomplish the following three things in a test:

- Provide the program with inputs that exercise the test we are interested in.
- Execute the program to perform the test.
- Examine the outputs to determine whether the test was successful.

## Example 4.13

### Condition testing with the branch testing strategy

Assume that the code below is what we meant to write.

```c
if (a || (b >= c)) { printf("OK\n"); }
```

The code that we mistakenly wrote instead follows:

```c
if (a && (b >= c)) { printf("OK\n"); }
```

If we apply branch testing to the code we wrote, one of the tests will use these values: a = 0, b = 3, c = 2 (making a false and b >= c true). In this case, the code should print the OK term [0 || (3 >= 2) is true] but instead doesn't print [0 && (3 >= 2) evaluates to false]. That test picks up the error.

Let's consider another more subtle error that is nonetheless all too common in

C. The code we meant to write follows:

```c
if ((x == good_pointer) && (x->field1 == 3))
{ printf("got the value\n"); }
```

Here is the bad code we actually wrote:

```c
if ((x = good_pointer) && (x->field1 == 3))
{ printf("got the value\n"); }
```

The problem here is that we typed = rather than ==, creating an assignment rather than a test. The code x = good_pointer first assigns the value good_pointer to x and then, because assignments are also expressions in C, returns good_pointer as the result of evaluating this expression.

If we apply the principles of branch testing, one of the tests we want to use will contain x != good_pointer and x ->field1 == 3. Whether this test catches the error depends on the state of the record pointed to by good_pointer. If it is equal to 3 at the time of the test, the message will be printed erroneously. Although this test is not guaranteed to uncover the bug, it has a reasonable chance of success. One of the reasons to use many different types of tests is to maximize the chance that supposedly unrelated elements will cooperate to reveal the error in a particular situation. Another more sophisticated strategy for testing conditionals is known as domain testing [How82], illustrated in Figure 5.28. Domain testing concentrates on linear inequalities. In the figure, the inequality the program should use for the test is j

<= i + 1. We test the inequality with three test points—two on the boundary of the valid region and a third outside the region but between the i values of the other two points. When we make some common mistakes in typing the inequality, these three tests are sufficient to uncover them, as shown in the figure.

### *Black-Box Testing*

Black-box tests are generated without knowledge of the code being tested. When used alone,black-box tests have a low probability of finding all the bugs in a program. But when used in conjunction with clear-box tests they help provide a well-rounded test set, since black-box tests are likely to uncover errors that are unlikely to be found by tests extracted from the code structure. Black-box tests can really work. For instance, when asked to test an instrument whose front panel was run by a microcontroller, one acquaintance of the author used his hand to depress all the buttons simultaneously. The front panel immediately locked up. This situation could occur in practice if the instrument were placed face-down on a table, but discovery of this bug would be very unlikely via clear-box tests.

One important technique is to take tests directly from the specification for the code under design. The specification should state which outputs are expected for certain inputs. Tests should be created that provide specified outputs and evaluate whether the results also satisfy the inputs. Random tests form one category of black-box test. Random values are generated with a given distribution. The expected values are computed independently of the system, and then the test inputs are applied. A large number of tests must be applied for the results to be statistically significant, but the tests are easy to generate. Another scenario is to test certain types of data values. For example, integer- valued inputs can be generated at interesting values such as 0, 1, and values near the maximum end of the data range. Illegal values can be tested as well.

Regression tests form an extremely important category of tests. When tests are created during earlier stages in the system design or for previous versions of the system, those tests should be saved to apply to the later versions of the system. Clearly, unless the system specification changed, the new system should be able to pass old tests. In some cases old bugs can creep back into systems, such as when an old version of a software module is inadvertently installed.

### *Evaluating Function Tests*

How much testing is enough? Horgan and Mathur [Hor96] evaluated the coverage of two well-known programs, TeX and awk. They used functional tests for these programs that had been developed over several years of extensive testing. Upon applying those functional tests to the programs, they obtained the code coverage statistics shown in Figure 5.30. The columns refer to various types of test coverage: block refers to basic blocks, decision to conditionals, p-use to a use of a variable in a predicate (decision), and c-use to variable use in a nonpredicate computation. These results are at least suggestive that functional testing does not fully exercise the code and that techniques that explicitly generate tests for various pieces of code are necessary to obtain adequate levels of code coverage.

Methodological techniques are important for understanding the quality of your tests. For example, if you keep track of the number of bugs tested each day, the data you collect over time should show you some trends on the number of errors per page of code to expect on the average, how many bugs are caught by certain kinds of tests, and so on. We address methodological approaches to quality control in more detail in Section 9.5. One interesting method for analyzing the coverage of your tests is error injection. First, take your existing code and add bugs to it, keeping track of where the bugs were added. Then run your existing tests on the modified program.

## Software Modem

In this section we design a modem. Low-cost modems generally use specialized chips, but some PCs implement the modem functions in software. Before jump- ing into the modem design itself, we discuss principles of how to transmit digital data over a telephone line. We will then go through a specification and discuss architecture, module design, and testing.

### *Theory of Operation and Requirements*

The modem will use frequency-shift keying (FSK),a technique used in 1200-baud modems. Keying alludes to Morse code-style keying. As shown in Figure the FSK scheme transmits sinusoidal tones, with 0 and 1 assigned to different frequencies. Sinusoidal tones are much better suited to transmission over analog phone lines than are the traditional high and low voltages of digital circuits. The 01 bit pat- terns create the chirping sound characteristic of moems. (Higher-speed modems, The modem will not implement a hardware interface to a telephone line or software for dialing a phone number. We will assume that we have analog audio inputs and outputs for sending and receiving. We will also run at a much slower bit rate than 1200 baud to simplify the implementation. Next, we will not implement a serial interface to a host, but rather put the transmitter's message in memory and save the receiver's result in memory as well. Given those understandings, let's fill out the requirements table. Start bit
Bit

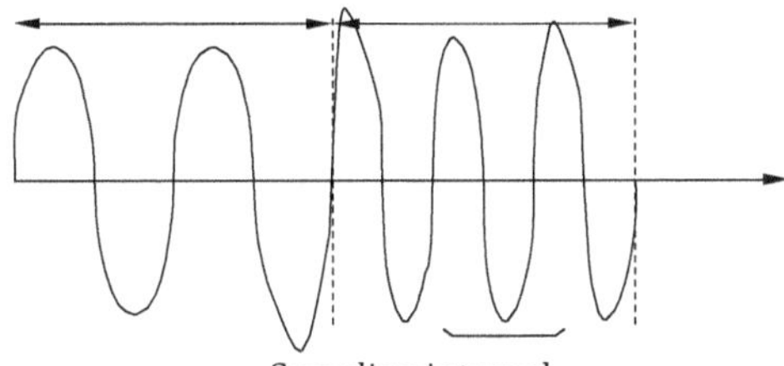
Sampling interval

Receiving bits  in the   modem. Name Modem. Purpose A fixed baud rate frequency-shift keyed  modem. Inputs Analog sound input, reset button.

Outputs     Analog  sound  output, LED bit display.

Functions Transmitter: Sends dat a stored   in  microprocessor memory  in 8-bit bytes. Sends start  bit  for each  byte equal  in length  to one bit.

Receiver:  Automatically  detect bytes andstores results in main memory.

Displays currently received bit  on  LED.

Performance 1200  baud.

Manufacturing  cost Dominated  by microprocessor and analog I/O. Power Powered by AC through a standard  power  supply.

Physical  size and weight Small and  light  enough to fit on a desktop.

### *System Architecture*

The modem consists of one small subsystem (the Interrupt handlers for the samples) and two major subsystems (transmitter and receiver).Two sample interrupt handlers  are required, one for input  and  another  for output, but  they  are  very  simple. The transmitter is simpler, so let's  consider its software architecture  first.

```
float sine_wave[N_SAMP]
{ 0.0,  0.5,  0.866, 1,
  0.866, 0.5, 0.0, –0.5,
```

### *Analog Waveform and Samples*

The  best  way  to  generate  waveforms that retain  the  proper  shape  over  long  intervals  is table  lookup. Software oscillators can  be  used  to  generate  periodic  signals, but  numerical problems limit their accuracy. Figure 5.35 shows  an analog waveform with  sample  points and the C code for these samples. Table lookup can  be combined  with interpolation  to  generate high-resolution  waveforms  without excessive memory costs, which  is  more  accurate  than oscillators because no feed- back is  involved. The required  number  of samples for the modem can be found by experimentation with the analog/digital converter and the sampling code of the receiver is considerably more complex. The filters and detectors of Figure 5.33 can be implemented with circular buffers. But that module must feed a state machine that recognizes the bits. The recognizer state machine must use a timer to determine when to start and stop computing the filter output average based on the starting point of the bit. It must then determine the nature of the bit at the proper interval. It must also detect the start bit and measure it using the counter. The receiver sample interrupt handler is a natural candidate to double as the receiver timer since the receiver's time points are relative to samples. The hardware architecture is relatively simple. In addition to the analog/digital and digital/analog converters, a timer is required. The amount of memory required to implement the algorithms is relatively small.

### *Component Design and Testing*

The transmitter and receiver can be tested relatively thoroughly on the host platform since the timing-critical code only delivers data samples. The transmitter's output is relatively easy to verify, particularly if the data are plotted. A testbench can be constructed to feed the receiver code sinusoidal inputs and test its bit recognition rate. It is a good idea to test the bit detectors first before testing the complete receiver operation. One potential problem in host-based testing of the receiver is encountered when library code is used for the receiver function. If a DSP library for the target processor is used to implement the filters, then a substitute must be found or built for the host processor testing. The receiver must then be retested when moved to the target system to ensure that it still functions properly with the library code.

### *System Integration and Testing*

There are two ways to test the modem system: by having the modem's transmitter send bits to its receiver, and or by connecting two different modems. The ultimate test is to connect two different modems, particularly modems designed by different people to be sure that incompatible assumptions or errors were not made. But single-unit testing, called loop-back testing in the telecommunications industry, is simpler and a good first step. Loop-back can be performed in two ways. First, a shared variable can be used to directly pass data from the transmitter to the receiver. Second, an audio cable can be used to plug the analog output to the analog input. In this case it is also possible to inject analog noise to test the resiliency of the detection algorithm.

<h1 style="text-align:center">Unit-5</h1>

<h2 style="text-align:center">Real Time Operating System(RTOS) Based Design</h2>

The process and the operating system (OS). Together, these two abstractions let us switch the state of the processor between multiple tasks. The process cleanly defines the state of an executing pro- gram, while the OS provides the mechanism for switching execution between the  processes. These two mechanisms together let us build applications with more complex functionality and much greater flexibility to  satisfy  timing  requirements. The need to  satisfy complex  timing  requirements-events  happening  at  very different rates, intermittent events, and so on-causes us to use processes  and OSs to build embedded software.  Satisfying  complex timing  tasks   can  introduce  extremely  complex  control  into  programs.  Using  processes  to compartmentalize  functions  and  encapsulating  in  the  OS  the   control required to switch between processes make it much easier to satisfy timing requirements with  relatively clean control  within the  processes.

We are particularly interested in real-time operating  systems (RTOSs),which are OSs that provide facilities for satisfying real-time requirements. A RTOS allocates resources using algorithms that take real time into account. General-purpose OSs, in contrast, generally allocate resources using other criteria like fairness. Trying to allocate the  CPU equally to  all  processes without  regard  to  time  can  easily  cause processes to miss  their  deadlines. In the  next section, we  will  introduce  the  concepts  of  task  and process. Section  6.2  looks at how the RTOS implements processes   Section 6.3 develops algorithms for scheduling those processes  to  meet real-time requirements. Section 6.4 introduces some basic concepts in interprocess communication. Section 6.5 considers the performance of RTOSs while Section 6.6 looks  at power consumption.

## Multiple Tasks and Multiple Processes

Most embedded systems require functionality and timing that  is  too complex to embody in a single  program. We break  the  system  into multiple tasks in order to manage when things happen. In this section we will develop the basic abstractions that will be manipulated by the RTOS to build multirate systems.

### Tasks and Processes

Many (if not most) embedded computing systems do more than one thing—that is, the environment can  cause  mode  changes  that  in turn cause the embedded system to behave quite differently. For example, when designing a telephone answering machine, we can define recording a phone call and operating the user's control panel as distinct tasks, because they perform logically distinct operations and they must be performed at very different rates. These different tasks are part of the system's functionality, but that application-level organization of functionality is often reflected in the structure of the program as well.

A process is a single execution of a program. If we run the same program two different times, we have created two different processes. Each process has its own state that includes not only its registers but all of its memory. In some OSs, the memory management unit is used to keep each process in a separate address space. In others, particularly lightweight RTOSs, the processes run in the same address space. Processes that share the same address space are often called threads. To understand why the separation of an application into tasks may be reflected in the on the compression algorithm we implemented in Section 3.7. As shown in Figure 6.1, this device is connected to serial ports on both ends. The input to the box is an uncompressed stream of bytes. The box emits a compressed string of bits on the output serial line, based on a predefined compression table. Such a box may be used, for example, to compress data being sent to a modem.

The program's need to receive and send data at different rates—for example, the program may emit 2 bits for the first byte and then 7 bits for the second byte— will obviously find itself reflected in the structure of the code. It is easy to create irregular, ungainly code to solve this problem; a more elegant solution is to create a queue of output bits, with those bits being removed from the queue and sent to the serial port in 8-bit sets. But beyond the need to create a clean data structure that simplifies the control structure of the code, we must also ensure that we process the inputs and outputs at the proper rates. For example, if we spend too much time in packaging and emitting output characters, we may drop an input character. Solving timing problems is a more challenging problem.

## RTOS

A real-time operating system (RTOS) is an operating system that guarantees a certain capability within a specified time constraint. For example, an operating system might be designed to ensure that a certain object was available for a robot on an assembly line. In what is usually called a "hard" real-time operating system, if the calculation could not be performed for making the object available at the designated time, the operating system would terminate with a failure. In a "soft" real-time operating system, the assembly line would continue to function but the production output might be lower as objects failed to appear at their designated time, causing the robot to be temporarily unproductive. Some real-time operating systems are created for a special application and others are more general purpose. Some existing general purpose operating systems claim to be a real-time operating systems. To some extent, almost any general purpose operating hardware. Usually, the kernel is the first of the user-installed software on a computer, booting directly after the BIOS. Operating system kernels are specific to the hardware on which they are running, thus most operating systems are distributed with different kernel options that are configured when the system is installed. Changing major hardware components such as the motherboard, processor, or memory, often requires a kernel update. Additionally, often new kernels are offered that improve system security or performance. The two major types of kernels competing in today's computer markets are the Windows kernel and the unix-like kernels.

The Windows kernel is available only with the Microsoft Windows series of operating systems. It is proprietary software, developed and distributed by Microsoft Corporation. Introduced in Windows/386, it's many incarnations have since gone by several different names, and some had no names at all. The latest version of the Windows kernel was introduced in Windows NT, and has had many of it's functions removed and placed in user-mode software for Windows Vista. This leads to increased system stability and security. In Vista, application-level software exploits have much less access to the core functions of the operating system, and application crashes will not bring down the OS.

Unix-like kernels are a family of operating system kernels that are based upon, or operate similar to, the original Bell Labs UNIX operating system. Common examples of unix-like kernels are the Linux kernel, BSD, Mac OS, and Solaris. While many of these kernels were developed with original Bell Labs code as part of the software, not all of them have direct lineage to Bell. Linux, for instance, was developed as a free alternative to Minix, itself an independently developed variation of UNIX. Although originally running an original kernel design, Mac OS was outfitted with a unix-like kernel in 1988 with the introduction of A/UX. All subsequent Apple operating systems have unix-like kernels, including the current Mac OS-X's BSD-derived kernel.

### Definition

The kernel is the essential center of a computer operating system, the core that provides basic services for all other parts of the operating system. A synonym is nucleus. A kernel can be contrasted with a shell, the outermost part of an operating system that interacts with user commands. Kernel and shell are terms used more frequently in Unix operating systems than in IBM mainframe or Microsoft Windows systems.

Typically, a kernel (or any comparable center of an operating system) includes an interrupt handler that handles all requests or completed I/O operations that compete for the kernel's services, a scheduler that determines which programs share the kernel's processing time in what order, and a supervisor that actually gives use of the computer to each process when it is scheduled. A kernel may also include a manager of the operating system's address spaces in memory or storage, sharing these among all components and other users of the kernel's services. A kernel's services are requested by other parts of the operating system or by application programs through a specified set of program interfaces sometimes known as system calls. Because the code that makes up the kernel is needed continuously, it is usually loaded into computer storage in an area that is protected so that it will not be overlaid with other less frequently used parts of the operating system.

## Task

Task is "an execution path through address space". In other words, a set of program instruction s is loaded in memory. The address registers have been loaded with the initial address of the program. At the next clock cycle , the CPU will start execution, in accord with the program. The sense is  that some part of 'a plan is being accomplished'. As long as the program remains in this part of  the All this information should be stored at specific locations within the TSS

### *Define Task*

Task is a typically and infinite loop function this is called task.

A task oriented operating system is defined as an operating system concept that refers to the combination of a program being executed and bookkeeping information used by the operating system. Whenever you execute a program, the operating system creates a new task for it. The task is like an envelope for the program: it identifies the program with a task number and attaches other bookkeeping information to it. Many operating systems, including UNIX, OS/2, and Windows, are capable of running many tasks at the same time and are called multitasking operating systems.

In most operating systems, there is a one-to-one relationship between the task and the program, but some operating systems allow a program to be divided into multiple tasks. Such systems are called multithreading operating systems. An operating system concept that refers to the combination of a program being executed and bookkeeping information used by the operating system. Whenever you execute a program, the operating system creates a new task for it. The task is like an envelope for the program: it identifies the program with a task number and attaches other bookkeeping information to it.

The terms task and process are often used interchangeably, although some operating systems make a distinction between the two.

### Task Scheduling Algorithm

The assignment of start and end times to a set of tasks, subject to certain constraints. Constraints are typically either time constraints (the payload must be installed before the payload bay doors are closed) or resource constraints (this task requires a small crane and a crane operator). In the case where the tasks are programs to run concurrently on a computer, this is also known as multitasking.

### Task Interfaces to Each Other

The only multitasking problem that multitasked systems have to solve is that they cannot use the same data or hardware at the same time. There are two notably successful designs for coping with this problem:

- Semaphore
- Message passing

A semaphore is either locked, or unlocked. When locked a queue of tasks wait for the semaphore. Problems with semaphore designs are well known: priority inversion and deadlocks . In priority inversion, a high priority task waits because a low priority task has a semaphore. A typical solution is to have the task that has a semaphore run at the priority of the highest waiting task. In a  deadlock, two tasks lock two semaphores, but in the opposite order. This is usually solved by careful design, implementing queues, or by having floored semaphores (which pass control of a registers with the values from the PCB of the new process.

### Location of the PCB

Since the PCB contains the critical information for the process, it must be kept in an area of memory protected from normal user access. In some operating systems the PCB is placed in the beginning of the kernel stack of the process since that is a convenient protected location. Task Control Block - The Task Control Block (TCB) specifies all the parameters necessary to schedule and execute a routine.  Typically, a TCB is a 6-10 words long and is logically divided into two parts:

**Task-Independent Parameters** - The first four words (32-bit) of the TCB are task-independent and simply specify the scheduling parameters to the DSP scheduler.

**Task-Dependent Parameters** - These parameters specify the routine to be executed and the parameters of execution. The number and format of these parameters is routine dependent.

TCB's may be linked in a chain from one to another so that a single call to the DSP scheduler can place many tasks in the scheduler queue simultaneously. This has the side benefit of guaranteeing the relative synchronization of all the tasks in the TCB chain. The sequence of execution of tasks in a TCB chain can be controlled by assigning an appropriate priority to each task, if desired.

## Multitasking

In computing, multitasking is a method by which multiple tasks, also known as processes, share common processing resources such as a CPU. In the case of a computer with a single CPU, only one task is said to be running at any point in time, meaning that the CPU is actively executing instructions for that task. Multitasking solves the problem by scheduling which task may be the one running at any given time, and when another waiting task gets a turn. The act of reassigning a CPU from one task to another one is called a context switch. When context switches occur frequently enough the illusion of parallelism is achieved. Even on computers with more than one CPU (called multiprocessor machines), multitasking allows many more tasks to be run than there are CPUs. Operating systems may adopt one of many different scheduling strategies, which generally fall into the following categories:

- In multiprogramming systems, the running task keeps running until it performs an operation that requires waiting for an external event (e.g. reading from a tape) or until the computer's scheduler forcibly swaps the running task out of the CPU. Multiprogramming systems are designed to maximize CPU usage.
- In time-sharing systems, the running task is required to relinquish the CPU, either voluntarily or by an external event such as a hardware interrupt. Time sharing systems are designed to allow several programs to execute apparently simultaneously. The expression 'time sharing' was usually used to designate computers shared by interactive users at terminals, such as IBM's TSO, and VM/CMS
- In real-time systems, some waiting tasks are guaranteed to be given the CPU when an external event occurs. Real time systems are designed to control mechanical devices such as industrial robots, which require timely processing.
  The term *time-sharing* is no longer commonly used, having been replaced by simply multitasking, and by the advent of personal computers and workstations rather

than shared

- Preemptive multitasking allows the computer system to more reliably guarantee each process a regular "slice" of operating time. It also allows the system to rapidly deal with important external events like incoming data, which might require the immediate attention of one or another process.

## *Time Slice*

- The period of time for which a process is allowed to run in a preemptive multitasking system is generally called the time slice, or quantum. The scheduler is run once every time slice to choose the next process to run. If the time slice is too short then the scheduler will consume too much processing time.
- An interrupt is scheduled to allow the operating system kernel to switch between processes when their time slices expire, effectively allowing the processor's time to be shared between a number of tasks, giving the illusion that it is dealing with these tasks simultaneously, or concurrently. The operating system which controls such a design is called a multi-tasking system.

## *Systems Supporting Preemptive Multitasking*

- Examples of preemptive operating systems include AmigaOS, the Windows NT family (including XP, Vista, and Seven), Linux, *BSD, OS/2 2.X - OS/2 Warp 3 - 4.5, Mac OS X and Windows 95/98/ME (32-bit applications only). Unix and Unix-based systems, and VMS, as well as other systems used in the academic and medium-to-large business markets, have always supported preemptive multitasking, but for a long time were beyond the reach of most users either because of the costs of licensing or the expensive hardware required to support them.
- Examples of older, non-preemptive (cooperative) operating systems include Windows 1.x, 2.x, 3.x, Windows for Workgroups, Windows 95/98 (when running 16-bit applications), NetWare, and Classic Mac OS versions (system 5.0 and up). Non-multitasking operating systems include older versions of Mac OS, MS DOS, and Commodore 64 OS which could only execute one program at a time.

Amiga OS, based on the preemptive multitasking TRIPOS system, was the first such system widely available to home users (1985); though some contemporary systems had access to Unix- like systems such as Xenix and Coherent, they could often be prohibitively expensive for home use. Running on Motorola 68000-based Amiga systems without memory management, the system used dynamic loading of relocatable code blocks ("hunks" in Amiga jargon) to preemptively multitask all processes in the same flat address space.

Early PC operating systems such as MS-DOS and DR-DOS, did not support multitasking at all. Novell NetWare, Microsoft Windows and OS/2 systems introduced cooperative multitasking to the PC, but did not support preemptive multitasking. In the case of the PC, the slow start was partly because of the need to support a large legacy code base of DOS software written to run in single- user mode on a 8086-based PC, whereas the Amiga system was designed to multitask from the beginning.

### Nonpreemptive Multitasking

Nonpreemptive multitasking is a style of computer multitasking in which the operating system never initiates a context switch from a running process to another process. Such systems are either statically scheduled, most often periodic systems, or exhibit some form of cooperative multitasking, in which case the computational tasks can self-interrupt and voluntarily give control to other tasks. When non preemptive is used, a process that receives such resources can not be interrupted until it is finished. Available, the system performs a context switch. The steps in a context switch are:

1. Save the context of the thread that just finished executing.
2. Place the thread that just finished executing at the end of the queue for its priority.
3. Find the highest priority queue that contains ready threads.
4. Remove the thread at the head of the queue, load its context, and execute it.

The following classes of threads are not ready threads.

- Threads created with the CREATE_SUSPENDED flag
- Threads halted during execution with the SuspendThread or SwitchToThread function
- Threads waiting for a synchronization object or input.

Until threads that are suspended or blocked become ready to run, the scheduler does not allocate any processor time to them, regardless of their priority. The most common reasons for a context switch are:

- The time slice has elapsed.
- A thread with a higher priority has become ready to run.
- A running thread needs to wait.

When a running thread needs to wait, it relinquishes the remainder of its time slice.

### Context Switch

A context switch is the computing process of saving and restoring the state (context) of a CPU such that multiple processes can share a single CPU resource. The context switch is an essential feature of a multitasking operating system.

Context switches are usually time consuming and much of the design of operating systems is to minimize the time of context switches.

A context switch can mean a register context switch, a task context switch, a thread context switch, or a process context switch. What will be switched is determined by the processor and the operating system. The scheduler is the part of the operating systems that manage context switching, it perform context switching in one of the following conditions:

**Multitasking:** One process needs to be switched out of (termed "yield" which means "give up") the CPU so another process can run. Within a preemptive multitasking operating system, the scheduler allows every task (according to its priority level) to run for some certain amount of time, called its time slice where a timer interrupt triggers the operating system to schedule another process for execution instead. If a process will wait for one of the computer resources or will perform an I/O operation, the operating system schedules another process for execution instead.

Suspended the execution of the first process, it can now load the PCB and context of the second process. In doing so, the program counter from the PCB is loaded, and thus execution can continue in the new process. New processes are chosen from a queue or queues. Process and thread priority can influence which process continues execution, with processes of the highest priority checked first for ready threads to execute.

### Context Switch Definition

A context switch (also sometimes referred to as a process switch or a task switch) is the switching of the CPU (central processing unit) from one process or thread to another.

A process (also sometimes referred to as a task) is an executing (i.e., running) instance of a program. In Linux, threads are lightweight processes that can run in parallel and share an address space (i.e., a range of memory locations) and other resources with their parent processes (i.e., the processes that created them).

A context is the contents of a CPU's registers and program counter at any point in time. A register is a small amount of very fast memory inside of a CPU (as opposed to the slower RAM main memory outside of the CPU) that is used to speed the execution of computer programs by providing quick access to commonly used values, generally those in the midst of a calculation. A program counter is a specialized register that indicates the position of the CPU in its instruction sequence and which holds either the address of the instruction being executed or the address of the next instruction to be executed, depending on the specific system. Context switching can be described in slightly more detail as the kernel (i.e., the core of the operating system) performing the following activities with regard to processes (including threads) on the CPU: suspending the progression of one process and storing the CPU's state (i.e., the context) for that process somewhere in memory, retrieving the context of the next process from memory and restoring it in the CPU's registers and returning to the location indicated by the program counter (i.e., returning to the line of code at whichthe  process  was  interrupted)  in order to resume the process.

A context switch is sometimes described as the kernel suspending execution of one process on the CPU and resuming execution of some other process that had previously been suspended. Although this wording can help clarify the concept, it can be confusing in itself because a process is, by definition, an executing instance of a program. Thus the wording suspending progression of a process might be preferable.

### Context Switches and Mode Switches

Context switches can occur only in kernel mode. Kernel mode is a privileged mode of the CPU in which only the kernel runs and which provides access to all memory locations and all other system resources. Other programs, including applications, initially operate in user mode, but they can run portions of the kernel code via system calls. A system call is a request in a Unix-like operating system by an active process (i.e., a process currently progressing in the CPU) for a service performed by the kernel, such as input/output (I/O) or process creation (i.e., creation of a new 2.4 kernel.

One major advantage claimed for software context switching is that, whereas the hardware mechanism saves almost all of the CPU state, software can be more selective and save only that portion that actually needs to be saved and reloaded. However, there is some question as to how important this really is in increasing the efficiency of context switching. Its advocates also claim that software context switching allows for the possibility of improving the switching code, thereby further enhancing efficiency, and that it permits better control over the validity of the data that is being loaded.

## Scheduler

### What is the Scheduler?

The "task scheduler" (or often "scheduler") is the part of the software that schedules which task to run next. The scheduler is the part of the software that chooses which task to run next.

The scheduler is arguably the most difficult component of an RTOS to implement. Schedulers maintain a table of the current state of each task on the system, as well as the current priority of each task. The scheduler needs to manage the timer too.

### In general, there are 3 states that a task can be in:

**Active**. There can be only 1 active thread on a given processor at a time.

**Ready.** This task is ready to execute, but is not currently executing.

**Blocked**. This task is currently waiting on a lock or a critical section to become free.

### Some Systems Even Allow for Other States

Sleeping. The task has voluntarily given up control for a certain period of time.

Low-Priority. This task only runs when all other tasks are blocked or sleeping.

### There Are 2 ways the Scheduler is Called

- The current task voluntarily yield()s to the scheduler, calling the scheduler directly, or
- The current task has run "long enough", the timer hardware interrupts it, and the timer interrupt routine calls the scheduler.

The scheduler must save the current status of the current task (save the contents of all registers to a specified location), it must look through the list of tasks to find the highest priority task in the Ready state, and then must switch control back to that task (by restoring it's register values from memory). The scheduler should first check to ensure that it is enabled. If the scheduler is disabled, it shouldn't preempt the current thread. This can be accomplished by checking a current global flag value. Some functions will want to disable the scheduler, so this flag should be accessable by some accessor method. An alternate method to maintaining a global flag is simply to say that any function that wants to disable the scheduler can simply disable the timer. This way the scheduler never gets called, and never has to check any flags.

The scheduler is generally disabled inside a critical section, where we do not want to OS to preempt the current thread. Otherwise, the scheduler should remain active.

# Task Synchronization

## *Mutual Exclusion?*

Mutual exclusion (often abbreviated to mutex) algorithms are used in concurrent programming to avoid the simultaneous use of a common resource, such as a global variable, by pieces of computer code called critical sections. A critical section is a piece of code where a process or thread accesses.

## *Semaphore*

In computer science, a semaphore is a protected variable or abstract data type which constitutes the classic method for restricting access to shared resources such as shared memory in a parallel programming environment. A counting semaphore is a counter for a set of available resources, rather than a locked/unlocked flag of a single resource. Semaphores are the classic solution to preventing race conditions in the dining philosophers problem, although they do not prevent resource deadlocks

## *Introduction*

Semaphores can only be accessed using the following operations. Those marked atomic should not be interrupted (that is, if the system decides that the "turn is up" for the program doing this, it shouldn't stop it in the middle of those instructions) for the reasons explained below.

procedure V (S : Semaphore); begin

(* Increases the value of its argument semaphore by 1;

this increase is to be regarded as an indivisible operation, atomic. *)

S := S + 1;

end;

procedure P (S : Semaphore); begin

(* Decreases the value of its argument semaphore by 1 as soon as the resulting value would be non-negative. This operation is

to be regarded as indivisible, atomic. *) repeat

Wait(); until S > 0; S := S - 1;

end;

Notice that incrementing the variable S must not be interrupted, and the P operation must not be interrupted after S is found to be greater than 0. This can be done using a special instruction such as test-and-set (if the architecture's instruction set supports it), or (on uniprocessor systems) ignoring interrupts to prevent other processes from becoming active.

The value of a semaphore is the number of units of the resource which are free. (If there is only  one resource, a "binary semaphore" with values 0 or 1 is used.) The P operation busy-waits (uses its turn to do nothing) or maybe sleeps (tells the system not to give it a turn) until a resource is available, whereupon it immediately claims one. The V operation is the inverse; it simply makes a resource available again after the process has finished using it. The P and V operations must be atomic, which means that no process may ever be preempted in the middle of one of those operations to run another operation on the same semaphore.

The canonical names P and V come from the initials of Dutch words. The V stands for verhogen, or "increase". Several explanations have been given for P (including proberen for "to test", passeer for "pass", probeer "try", and pakken "grab"), but in fact Dijkstra wrote that he intended P to stand for the made-up word prolaag,short for probeer te verlagen, literally "try-to-reduce", or to parallel the terms used in the other case, "try-to-decrease". This confusion stems from the fact that the words for increase and decrease both begin with the letter V in Dutch, and the words spelled out in full would be impossibly confusing for non-Dutch-speakers.

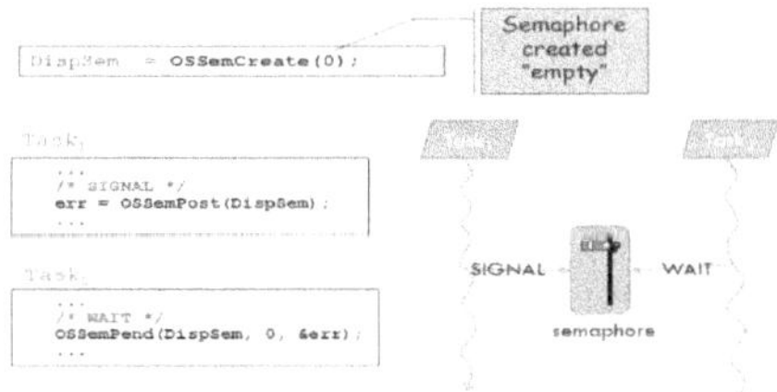


### Message Mail Boxes

### Intertask Communication

Information transfer is sometimes needed among tasks or between the task and the ISR. Information transfer can be also called intertask communication. There are two ways to implement it: through the global variable or by sending messages.

When using the global variable, it is important to ensure that each task or ISR possesses the variable alone. The only way to ensure it is enabling the interrupt. When two tasks share one variable, each task possesses the variable alone through firstly enabling then disabling the interrupt or by the semaphore. Please note that a task can communicate with the ISR only through the global variable and the task won't know when the global variable has been modified by the ISR (unless the ISR sends signals to the task in manner of semaphore or the task keeps searching the variable's value). In this case, CooCox CoOS supplies the mailboxes and the message queues to avoid the problems above.

Mailboxes

System or the user code can send a message by the core services. A typical mail message, also known as the exchange of information, refers to a task or an ISR using a pointer variable, through the core services to put a message (that is, a pointer) into the mailbox. Similarly, one or more tasks can receive this message by the core services. The tasks sending and receiving the message promise that the content that the pointer points to is just that piece of message.

The mailbox of CooCox CoOS is a typical message mailbox which is composed of two parts: one is the information which expressed by a pointer of void; the other is the waiting list which composed of the tasks waiting for this mailbox. The waiting list supports two kinds of sorting: FIFO and preemptive priority. The sorting mode is determined by the user when creating the mailbox.

You can create a mailbox by calling CoCreateMbox ( ) in CooCox CoOS. After being created successfully, there won't be any message inside. You can send a message to the mailbox by calling CoPostMail ( ) or isr_PostMail ( ) respectively in a task or the ISR. You can also get a message from the mailbox by calling CoPendMail ( ) or CoAcceptMail ( ). The use of the mailbox

*

void myTaskA(void* pdata)

{

void* pmail; StatusType err;

You can create a message queue by calling CoCreateQueue ( ) in CooCox CoOS. After being created successfully, there won't be any message inside. You can send a message to the message queue by calling CoPostQueueMail ( ) or isr_PostQueueMaill ( ) respectively in a task or the ISR. Similarly, you can also obtain a message from the message queue by calling CoPendQueueMail ( ) or CoAcceptQueueMail ( ).

# RTOS-BASED DESIGN-2

## Message Passing

Message passing communication complements the shared memory model. As shown in Figure 6.15, each communicating entity has its own message send/receive unit. The message is not stored on the communications link, but rather at the senders/receivers at the end points. In contrast, shared memory communication can be seen as a memory block used as a communication device, in which all the data are stored in the communication link/memory.

Applications in which units operate relatively autonomously are natural candidates for message passing communication. For example, a home control system has one microcontroller per household device—lamp, thermostat, faucet, appliance, and so on. The devices must communicate relatively infrequently; furthermore, their physical separation is large enough that we would not naturally think of them as sharing a central pool of memory. Passing communication packets among the devices is a natural way to describe coordination between these devices. Message passing is the natural implementation of communication in many 8-bit microcontrollers that do not normally operate with external memory.

## Signals

Another form of interprocess communication commonly used in Unix is the signal. A signal is simple because it does not pass data beyond the existence of the signal itself.

A signal is analogous to an interrupt, but it is entirely a software creation. A signal is generated by a process and transmitted to another process by the operating system.

A UML signal is actually a generalization of the Unix signal. While a Unix signal carries no parameters other than a condition code, a UML signal is an object.

As such, it can carry parameters as object attributes.

Figure 6.16 shows the use of a signal in UML. The sigbehavior( ) behavior of the class is responsible for throwing the signal, as indicated by send . The signal object is indicated by the signal stereotype.

## Evaluating Operating System Performance

The scheduling policy does not tell us all that we would like to know about the performance of a real system running processes.

Our analysis of scheduling policies makes some simplifying assumptions:

- We have assumed that context switches require zero time. Although it is often reasonable to neglect context switch time when it is much smaller than the process execution time, context switching can add significant delay in some cases.

Determine when to take actions. However, the overall strategy embodied in the policy should be designed based on the characteristics of the static and dynamic power management mechanisms. Going into a low-power mode takes time; generally, the more that is shut off, the longer the delay incurred during restart. Because power-down and power-up are not free, modes should be changed carefully. Determining when to switch into and out of a power-up mode requires an analysis of the overall system activity.

- Avoiding a power-down mode can cost unnecessary power.
- Powering down too soon can cause severe performance penalties.
- Re-entering run mode typically costs a considerable amount of time.

A straightforward method is to power up the system when a request is received. This works as long as the delay in handling the request is acceptable. A more sophisticated technique is predictive shutdown. The goal is to predict when the next request will be made and to start the system just before that time, saving the requestor the start-up time. In general, predictive shutdown techniques are probabilistic-they make guesses about activity patterns based on a probabilistic model of expected behavior. Because they rely on statistics, they may not always correctly guess the time of the next activity. This can cause two types of problems:

- The requestor may have to wait for an activity period. In the worst case, the requestor may not make a deadline due to the delay incurred by system start-up.
- The system may restart itself when no activity is imminent. As a result, the system will waste power.

Clearly, the choice of a good probabilistic model of service requests is important. The policy mechanism should also not be too complex, since the power it consumes to make decisions is part of the total system power budget. Several predictive techniques are possible. A very simple technique is to use fixed times.

For instance, if the system does not receive inputs during an interval of length Ton, it shuts down; a powered-down system waits for a period Toff before returning to the

S1, a low wake-up latency state with no loss of system  context;

S2, a low wake-up latency state with a loss of CPU and system cache state;

S3, a low wake-up latency state in which all system state except for main memory  is lost;  and

S4, the lowest-power sleeping state, in which all devices are turned off.

- G1, the sleeping state, in which the system appears to be off and the time required to return  to working condition is inversely proportional to power consumption.

## Telephone Answering Machine

In this section we design a digital telephone answering machine. The system will store messages in digital form rather than on an analog tape.  To make life more interesting, we use a simple algorithm to compress the voice data so that we can make more efficient use of the limited amount of available memory.

### *Theory of Operation and Requirements*

In addition to studying the compression algorithm, we also need to learn a little about the operation of telephone systems. The compression scheme we will use is known as adaptive differential pulse code modulation (ADPCM). Despite the long name, the technique is relatively simple but can yield 2 compression ratios on voice data. The ADPCM coding scheme is illustrated in Unlike traditional sampling, in which each sample shows the magnitude of the signal at a particular time, ADPCM encodes changes in the signal. The samples are expressed in a coding alphabet, whose values are in a relative range  that spans both negative and positive values.  In this case, the value range is { 3, 2, 1, 1, 2, 3}. Each sample is used to predict the value of the signal at the current instant from the previous value. At each point in time, the sample is chosen such that the error between the predicted value and the actual signal value is minimized. An ADPCM compression system, including an encoder and decoder, is shown in Figure but the terminology  starts to make sense after a few uses.) Our interface will send  a digital signal to take the phone line off-hook, which will cause analog circuitry to make the necessary connection so that  voice  data  can be sent  and received  during the  call. We can now write the requirements for the answering machine. We will assume that the interface is not to the actual phone line but to some circuitry that provides voice samples, off-hook commands, and so on. Such circuitry will let us test our system with a telephone line simulator and then build  the analog circuitry necessary to connect to a real phone line. We will use the term outgoing message (OGM) to refer to the message recorded by the owner  of the machine and played at the start of every  phone   call.

| Name | Digital telephone answering machine |
| --- | --- |

Telephone answering machine with digital memory, using speech compression. Inputs

*Telephone:* voice samples, ring indicator.
User interface: microphone, play messages button, record OGM but

Telephone: voice samples, on-hook/off-hook command.

User interface: speaker, # messages indicator, message light.

Functions

Default mode: When machine receives ring indicator, it signals off-hook, plays the OGM, and then records the incoming message. Maximum recording length for incoming message is 30 s, at which time the machine hangs up. If the machine runs out of memory, the OGM is played and the machine then hangs up with- out recording.

Playback mode: When the play button is depressed, the machine plays all messages. If the play button is depressed again within five seconds, the messages are played again. Messages are erased after playback.

OGM editing mode: When the user hits the record OGM button, the machine records an OGM of up to

10 s. When the user holds down the record OGM but- ton and hits the play button, the OGM is played back. Performance Should  be able  to record  about  30 min of total voice, including incoming and OGMs. Voice data are sampled at the standard telephone rate of 8 kHz.

### *Specification*

The class diagram for the answering machine. In addition to the classes that perform the major functions, we also use classes to describe the incoming and OGMs. As seen below, user interface and the telephone interface. The user and telephone interfaces both appear internally as I/O devices on the CPU bus with the main memory serving as the storage for the messages. The software splits into the following seven major pieces:

- The front panel module handles the buttons and lights.

- The speaker module handles sending data to the user's speaker.

- The telephone line module handles off-hook detection and  on-hook commands.

- The telephone input and output modules handle receiving samples from and sending samples to the telephone line.

- The compression module compresses data and stores it in memory.

- The decompression module uncompresses data and sends it to the speaker module.

We can determine the execution model for these modules based on the rates at which they must work and the ways in which they communicate.

- The front panel and telephone line modules must regularly test the buttons and phone line, but this can be done at a fairly low rate. As seen below, they can therefore run as polled processes in the software's main loop.

  ```
  while (TRUE) { check_phone_line(); run_front_panel();
  }
  ```

- The speaker and phone input and output modules must run at higher, regular rates and are natural candidates for interrupt processing. These modules don't run all the time and so can be disabled by the front panel and telephone line modules when they are not needed.

- The compression and decompression modules run at the same rate as the speaker and telephone I/O modules, but they are not directly connected to devices. We will therefore call them as subroutines to the interrupt modules.

Idea. In the United States, the Federal Communications Commission regulates equipment connected to phone lines. Beyond legal problems, a bad circuit can damage the phone line and incur the wrath of your service provider. The required analog circuitry also requires some amount of tuning, and you need a second telephone line to generate phone calls for tests. You can build a telephone line simulator to test the hardware independently of a real telephone line.

# UNIT-7

## DISTRIBUTED EMBEDDED SYSTEMS

## Networks for Embedded Systems

Networks for embedded computing span a broad range of requirements; many of those requirements are very different from those for general-purpose networks. Some networks are used in safety-critical applications, such as automotive control. Some networks, such as those used in consumer electronics systems, must be very inexpensive. Other networks, such as industrial control networks, must be extremely rugged and reliable. Several interconnect networks have been developed especially for distributed embedded computing:

- The $I^2$ C bus is used in microcontroller-based systems.

- The Controller Area Network (CAN) bus was developed for automotive electronics. It provides megabit rates and can handle large numbers of devices.

- Ethernet and variations of standard. Ethernet are used for a variety of control applications.

In addition, many networks designed for general-purpose computing have been put to use in embedded applications as well. This section, we study some commonly used embedded networks, including the $I^2C$ bus and Ethernet; we will also briefly discuss networks for industrial applications.

### *The I²C Bus*

The*I $^2$C bus* [Phi92] is a well-known bus commonly used to link microcontrollers into systems. It has even been used for the command interface in an MPEG-2 video chip [van97]; while a separate bus was used for high-speed video data, setup information was interfering with another message.

Every $I^2C$ device has an address. The addresses of the devices are determined by the system designer, usually as part of the program for the $I^2$ C driver. The addresses must of course be chosen so that no two devices in the system have the same address. A device address is 7 bits in the standard $I^2C$ definition(the extended $I^2C$ allows 10-bit addresses). The address 0000000 is used to signal a general call or bus broadcast, which can be used to signal all devices simultaneously. The address 11110XX is reserved for the extended 10-bit addressing scheme; there are several other reserved addresses as well.

A bus transaction comprised a series of 1-byte transmissions and an address followed by one or more data bytes. $I^2C$ encourages a data-push programming style. When a master wants to write a slave, it transmits the slave's address followed by the data. Since a slave cannot initiate a  transfer, the master must send a read request with the slave's address and let the slave transmit the data. Therefore, an address transmission includes the 7-bit address and 1 bit for data direction: 0 for writing from the master to the slave and 1 for reading from the slave to the master. (This explains the 7-bit addresses on the bus.) The format of an address transmission is shown in Figure 8.9. A bus transaction is initiated by a start signal and completed with an end signal as follows:

- A start is signaled by leaving the SCL high and sending a 1 to 0 transition on SDL.

- A stop is signaled by setting the SCL high and sending a 0 to 1 transition on SDL.

However, starts and stops must be paired.  A master can write and then read(or read and then write) by sending a start after the data transmission, followed by another address transmission and  then more  data. The basic state transition graph for the master's actions in a bus transaction.

The formats of some typical complete bus transactions are shown in Figure 8.11. In the first example, the master writes 2 bytes to the addressed slave.  In the second, the master requests a read from a slave. In the third, the master writes 1 byte to the slave, and then sends another start to initiate a read from the slave. Transmitting a byte on the $I^2C$ bus.

### *Ethernet*

Ethernet is very widely used as a local area network for general-purpose computing. Because of its ubiquity and the low cost of Ethernet interfaces, it has seen significant use as a network for embedded computing. Ethernet is particularly useful when PCs are used as platforms, making it possible to use standard components, and when the network does not have to meet rigorous real-time requirements. The physical organization of an Ethernet is very simple, as shown in Figure. The network is a bus with a single signal path; the Ethernet standard allows for several different  implementations such as twisted pair and coaxial cable.

Unlike the $I^2$ C bus, nodes on the Ethernet are not synchronized-they can send their bits at any time. $I^2C$ relies on the fact that a collision can be detected and quashed within a single bit time thanks to synchronization. But since Ethernet nodes are not synchronized, if two nodes decide to transmit at the same time, the message will be ruined. The Ethernet arbitration scheme is known as Carrier Sense Multiple Access with Collision Detection (CSMA/CD). The algorithm is outlined in Figure 8.15. A node that has a message waits for the bus to become silent and then starts transmitting. It simultaneously listens, and if it hears another transmission that interferes with its transmission, it stops transmitting and waits to retransmit. The waiting time is random, but weighted by an exponential function of the number of times the message has been aborted. Figure 8.16 shows the exponential backoff function both before and after it is modulated by the random wait time. Since a message may be interfered with several times before it is successfully transmitted, the exponential backoff technique helps to ensure that the network does not become overloaded at high demand factors. The random factor in the wait time minimizes the chance that two messages will repeatedly interfere with each other.

The maximum length of an Ethernet is determined by the nodes' ability to detect collisions. The worst case occurs when two nodes at opposite ends of the bus are transmitting simultaneously. For the collision to be detected by both nodes, each node's signal must be able to travel to the opposite end of the bus so that it can be heard by the other node. In practice, Ethernets can run up to several hundred

## Network-Based Design

Designing a distributed embedded system around a network involves some of the same design tasks we faced in accelerated systems. We must schedule computations in time and allocate them to PEs. Scheduling and allocation of communication are important additional design tasks required for many distributed networks. Many embedded networks are designed for low cost and therefore do not provide excessively high communication speed. If we are not careful, the network can become the bottleneck in system design. In this section we concentrate on design tasks unique to network-based distributed embedded systems.

We know how to analyze the execution time of programs and systems of processes on single CPUs, but to analyze the performance of networks we must know how to determine the delay incurred by transmitting messages. Let us assume for the moment that messages are sent reliably-we do not have to retransmit a message. The message delay for a single message with no contention (as would be the case in a point-to-point connection) can be modeled as where $t_x$ is the transmitter-side overhead, $t_n$ is the network transmission time, and tr is the receiver-side overhead. In $I^2$ C, $t_x$ and $t_r$ are negligible relative to $t_n$, as illustrated. If the network uses fixed-priority arbitration, the network availability delay is unbounded for all but the highest-priority device. Since the highest-priority device always gets the network first, unless there is an application-specific limit on how long it will transmit before relinquishing the network, it can keep blocking the other devices indefinitely.

- If the network uses fair arbitration, the network availability delay is bounded. In the case of round-robin arbitration, if there are $N$ devices, then the worst- case network availability delay is $N$ $(t_x$ $t_{arb}$ $)$, where $t_{arb}$ is the delay incurred for arbitration. $t_{arb}$ is usually small compared to transmission time.

Even when round-robin arbitration is used to bound the network availability delay, the waiting time can be very long. If we add acknowledgment and data corruption into the analysis, figuring network delay is more difficult. Assuming that errors are random, we cannot predict a worst-case delay since every packet may contain an error. We can, however, compute the probability that a packet will be delayed for more than a given amount of time. However, such analysis is beyond the scope of this look.

Arbitration on networks is a form of prioritization. Therefore, we can use the techniques we learned for process scheduling in Chapter 6 to help us schedule communications. In a rate-monotonic communication scheme, the task with the shortest deadline should be assigned the highest priority in the network.

Our process scheduling model assumed that we could interrupt processes at any point. But network communications are organized into packets. In most networks we cannot interrupt a packet transmission to take over the network for a higher-priority packet.As a result, networks exhibit priority inversion like that introduced in Chapter 6. When a low-priority message is on the network, the network is effectively allocated to that low-priority message, allowing it to block higher-priority messages. This cannot cause deadlock since each message has a bounded length, but it can slow down critical communications. The only solution is to analyze network behavior to determine whether priority inversion causes some messages to be delayed for too long.

Of course, a round-robin arbitrated network puts all communications at the same priority. This does not eliminate the priority inversion problem because processes still have priorities.

Thus far we have assumed a single-hop network: A message is received at its intended destination directly from the source, without going through any other network node. It is possible to build multihop networks in which messages are routed through network nodes to get to their destinations. (Using a multistage network does not necessarily mean using a multihop network—the stages in a multistage network are generally much smaller than the network PEs.) Figure 8.18 shows an example of a multihop communication. The hardware platform has two separate networks ( perhaps so that communications between subsets of the PEs do not interfere), but there is no direct path from M 1 to M 5. The message is therefore routed through M3, which reads it from one network and sends it on to the other one. Analyzing delays

## Internet-enabled Systems

Some very different types of distributed embedded system are rapidly emerging-the Internet-enabled embedded system and Internet appliances. The Internet is not well suited to the real-time tasks that are the bread and butter of embedded computing, but it does provide a rich environment for non–real-time interaction. In this section we will discuss the Internet and how it can be used by embedded computing systems

### *Internet*

The Internet Protocol (IP) [Los97, Sta97A] is the fundamental protocol on the Internet. It provides connectionless, packet-based communication. Industrial automation has long been a good application area for Internet-based embedded systems. Information appliances that use the Internet are rapidly becoming another use of IP in embedded computing.

Internet protocol is not defined over a particular physical implementation-it is an internetworking standard. Internet packets are assumed to be carried by some other network, such as an Ethernet. In general, an Internet packet will travel over several different networks from source to destination. The IP allows data to flow seamlessly through these networks from one end user to another. The relationship between IP and individual networks is illustrated in Figure 8.19. IP works at the net- work layer. When node A wants to send data to node B, the application's data pass through several layers of the protocol stack to send to the IP. IP creates packets for routing to the destination, which are then sent to the data link and physical layers. A node that transmits data among different types of networks is known as a router. The router's functionality must go up to the IP layer, but since it is not running applications, it does not need to go to higher levels of the OSI model. In general, a packet may go through several routers to get to its destination. At the destination, the IP layer provides data to the transport layer and ultimately the receiving application. As the data pass through several layers of the protocol stack, the IP packet data are encapsulated in packet formats appropriate to each layer. The basic format of an IP packet is shown in Figure 8.20. The header and data payload are both of variable length. The maximum total length of the header and data payload is 65,535 bytes. An Internet address is a number (32 bits in early versions of IP, 128 bits in IPv6). The IP address is typically written in the form xxx.xx.xx.xx.The names by which users and applications typically refer to Internet nodes, such as foo.baz.com, The fact that IP works at the network layer tells us that it does not guarantee that a packet is delivered to its destination. Furthermore, packets that do arrive may come out of order. This is referred to as best-effort routing . Since routes for data may change quickly with subsequent packets being routed along very different paths with different delays, real-time performance of IP can be hard to predict. When a small network is contained totally within the embedded system, performance can be evaluated through simulation or other methods because the possible inputs are limited. Since the performance of the Internet may depend on worldwide usage patterns, its real-time performance is inherently harder to predict.

The Internet also provides higher-level services built on top of IP. The Transmission Control Protocol (TCP) is one such example. It provides a connection-oriented service that ensures that data arrive in the appropriate order, and it uses an acknowledgment protocol to ensure that packets arrive. Because many higher- level services are built on top of TCP, the basic protocol is often referred to as TCP/IP.

Wide Web service, Simple Mail Transfer Protocol for email, and Telnet for virtual terminals. A separate transport protocol, User Datagram Protocol, is used as

The Internet service stack. The basis for the network management services provided by the Simple Network

### *Management Protocol*

### *Internet Applications*

The Internet provides a standard way for an embedded system to act in concert with other devices and with users, such as:

- One of the earliest Internet-enabled embedded systems was the laser printer. High-end laser printers often use IP to receive print jobs from host machines.
- Portable Internet devices can display. Web pages, read email, and synchronize calendar information with remote computers.
- A home control system allows the homeowner to remotely monitor and control home cameras, lights, and so on.

Although there are higher-level services that provide more time-sensitive delivery mechanisms for the Internet, the basic incarnation of the Internet is not well suited to hard real-time operations. However, IP is a very good way to let the embedded system talk to other systems. IP provides a way for both special-purpose and standard programs (such as Web browsers) to talk to the embedded system. This non–real-time interaction can be used to monitor the system, set its configuration, and interact with it.

As seen in Section 8.4.1, the Internet provides a wide range of services built on top of IP. Since code size is an important issue in many embedded systems, one architectural decision that must be made is to determine which Internet services will be needed by the system. This choice depends on the type of data service required, such as connectionless versus connection oriented, streaming vs. non-streaming, and so on. It also depends on the application code and its services: does the system look to the rest of the Internet like a terminal, a Web server, or something else?

## Vehicles as Networks

Modern cars and planes rely on electronics to operate. About one-third of the total cost of an airplane or car comes from its electronics. Electronic systems are used in all aspects of the vehicle—safety-critical control, navigation and systems monitoring, and passenger comfort. These electronic devices are connected using data networks. Networks are used for a variety of purposes in vehicles, with varying requirements on reliability and performance:

- Vehicle control (steering and brakes in cars, flight control surfaces in airplanes) is the most critical operation in the vehicle since it determines vehicle stability.

# Unit-8

## Embedded Systems Development Environment

## The Integrated Development Environment

Integrated development environments are designed to maximize programmer productivity by providing tight-knit components with similar user interfaces. IDEs present a single program in which all development is done. This program typically provides many features for authoring, modifying, compiling, deploying and debugging software. This contrasts with software development using unrelated tools, such as vi, GCC or make.

One aim of the IDE is to reduce the configuration necessary to piece together multiple development utilities, instead providing the same set of capabilities as a cohesive unit. Reducing that setup time can increase developer productivity, in cases where learning to use the IDE is faster than manually integrating all of the individual tools. Tighter integration of all development tasks has the potential to improve overall productivity beyond just helping with setup tasks. For example, code can be continuously parsed while it is being edited, providing instant feedback when syntax errors are introduced. That can speed learning a new programming language and its associated libraries.

Some IDEs are dedicated to a specific programming language, allowing a feature set that most closely matches the programming paradigms of the language. However, there are many multiple-language IDEs, such as Eclipse, ActiveState Komodo, IntelliJ IDEA, Oracle JDeveloper, NetBeans, Codenvy and Microsoft Visual Studio. Xcode, Xojo and Delphi are dedicated to a closed language or set of programming languages.

While most modern IDEs are graphical, text-based IDEs such as Turbo Pascal were in popular use before the widespread availability of windowing systems like Microsoft Windows and the X Window System (X11). They commonly use function keys or hotkeys to execute frequently used commands or macros.

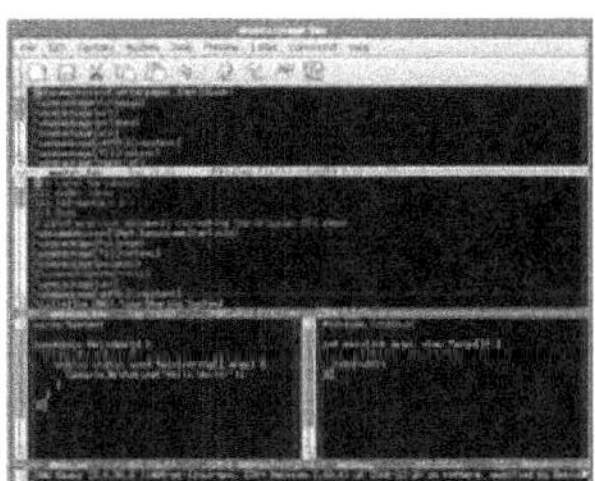

GNU Emacs, an extensible editor that is commonly used as an IDE on Unix-like systems. IDEs initially became possible when developing via a console or terminal. Early systems could not support one, since programs were prepared using flowcharts, entering programs with punched cards (or paper tape, etc.) before submitting them to a compiler. Dartmouth BASIC was the first language to be created with an IDE (and was also the first to be designed for use while sitting in front of a console or terminal). Its IDE (part of the Dartmouth Time Sharing System) was command-based, and therefore did not look much like the menu-driven, graphical IDEs prevalent today. However it integrated editing, file management, compilation, debugging and execution in a manner consistent with a modern IDE. Maestro I is a product from Softlab Munich and was the world's first integrated development environment[1] 1975 for software. Maestro I was installed for 22,000 programmers worldwide. Until 1989, 6,000 installations existed in the Federal Republic of Germany. Maestro I was arguably the world leader in this field during the 1970s and 1980s. Today one of the last Maestro I can be found in the Museum of Information Technology at Arlington. One of the first IDEs with a plug-in concept was Softbench. In 1995 Computerwoche commented that the use of an IDE was not well received by developers since it would fence in their creativity.

A cross compiler is a compiler capable of creating executable code for a platform other than the one on which the compiler is running. For example in order to compile for Linux/ARM you first need to obtain its libraries to compile against.

A cross compiler is necessary to compile for multiple platforms from one machine. A platform could be infeasible for a compiler to run on, such as for the microcontroller of an embedded system because those systems contain no operating system. In paravirtualization one machine runs many operating systems, and a cross compiler could generate an executable for each of them from one main source.

Cross compilers are not to be confused with a source-to-source compilers. A cross compiler is for cross-platform software development of binary code, while a source-to-source "compiler" just translates from one programming language to another in text code. Both are programming tools. Compiling for multiple machines. For example, a company may wish to support several different versions of an operating system or to support several different operating systems. By using a cross compiler, a single build environment can be set up to compile for each of these targets. Compiling on a server farm. Similar to compiling for multiple machines, a complicated build that involves many compile operations can be executed across any machine that is free, regardless of its underlying hardware or the operating system version that it is running.

Bootstrapping to a new platform. When developing software for a new platform, or the emulator of a future platform, one uses a cross compiler to compile necessary tools such as the operating system and a native compiler.

Compiling native code for emulators for older now-obsolete platforms like the Commodore 64 or Apple II by enthusiasts who use cross compilers that run on a current platform (such as Aztec C's MS-DOS 6502 cross compilers running under Windows XP). Use of virtual machines (such as Java's JVM) resolves some of the reasons for which cross compilers were developed. The virtual machine paradigm allows the same compiler output to be used across multiple target systems, although this is not always ideal because virtual machines are often slower and the compiled program can only be run on computers with that virtual machine.

Typically the hardware architecture differs (e.g. compiling a program destined for the MIPS architecture on an x86 computer) but cross-compilation is also applicable when only the operating system environment differs, as when compiling a FreeBSD program under Linux, or even just the system library, as when compiling programs with uClibc on a glibc host.

### *Canadian Cross*

The Canadian Cross is a technique for building cross compilers for other machines. Given three machines A, B, and C, one uses machine A (e.g. running Windows XP on an IA-32 processor) to build a cross compiler that runs on machine B (e.g. running Mac OS X on an x86-64 processor) to create executables for machine C (e.g. running Android on an ARM processor). When using the Canadian Cross with GCC, there may be four compilers involved:

The proprietary native Compiler for machine A (1) (e.g. compiler from Microsoft Visual Studio) is used to build the gcc native compiler for machine A (2).

The gcc native compiler for machine A (2) is used to build the gcc cross compiler from machine A to machine B (3)

The gcc cross compiler from machine A to machine B (3) is used to build the gcc cross compiler from machine B to machine C (4).

The end-result cross compiler (4) will not be able to run on your build machine A; instead you would use it on machine B to compile an application into executable code that would then be copied to machine C and executed on machine C.

For instance, NetBSD provides a POSIX Unix shell script named build.sh which will first build its own toolchain with the host's compiler; this, in turn, will be used to build the cross-compiler which will be used to build the whole system.

The term Canadian Cross came about because at the time that these issues were under discussion, Canada had three national political parties.

## What is a Disassembler?

In essence, a disassembler is the exact opposite of an assembler. Where an assembler converts code written in an assembly language into binary machine code, a disassembler reverses the process and attempts to recreate the assembly code from the binary machine code.

Since most assembly languages have a one-to-one correspondence with underlying machine instructions, the process of disassembly is relatively straight-forward, and a basic disassembler can often be implemented simply by reading in bytes, and performing a table lookup. Of course, disassembly has its own problems and pitfalls, and they are covered later in this chapter.

Many disassemblers have the option to output assembly language instructions in Intel, AT&T, or (occasionally) HLA syntax. Examples in this book will use Intel and AT&T syntax interchangeably. We will typically not use HLA syntax for code examples, but that may change in the future.

### *Disassembler Issues*

As we have alluded to before, there are a number of issues and difficulties associated with the disassembly process. The two most important difficulties are the division between code and data, and the loss of text information.

## Separating Code from Data

Since data and instructions are all stored in an executable as binary data, the obvious question arises: how can a disassembler tell code from data? Is any given byte a variable, or part of an instruction?

The problem wouldn't be as difficult if data were limited to the .data section (segment) of an executable (explained in a later chapter) and if executable code were limited to the .code section of an executable, but this is often not the case. Data may be inserted directly into the code section (e.g. jump address tables, constant strings), and executable code may be stored in the data section (although new systems are working to prevent this for security reasons). AI programs, LISP or Forth compilers may not contain .text and .data sections to help decide, and have code and data interspersed in a single section that is readable, writable and executable, Boot code may even require substantial effort to identify sections. A technique that is often used is to identify the entry point of an executable, and find all code reachable from there, recursively. This is known as "code crawling".

Many interactive disassemblers will give the user the option to render segments of code as either code or data, but non-interactive disassemblers will make the separation automatically. Disassemblers often will provide the instruction AND the corresponding hex data on the same line, shifting the burden for decisions about the nature of the code to the user. Some disassemblers (e.g. ciasdis) will allow you to specify rules about whether to disassemble as data or code and invent label names, based on the content of the object under scrutiny. Scripting your own "crawler" in this way is more efficient; for large programs interactive disassembling may be impractical to the point of being unfeasible.

The general problem of separating code from data in arbitrary executable programs is equivalent to the halting problem. As a consequence, it is not possible to write a disassembler that will correctly separate code and data for all possible input programs. Reverse engineering is full of such theoretical limitations, although by Rice's theorem all interesting questions about program properties are undecidable (so compilers and many other tools that deal with programs in any form run into such limits as well). In practice a combination of interactive and automatic analysis and perseverance can handle all but programs specifically designed to thwart reverse engineering, like using encryption and decrypting code just prior to use, and moving code around in memory.

## Lost Information

User defined textual identifiers, such as variable names, label names, and macros are removed by the assembly process. They may still be present in generated object files, for use by tools like debuggers and relocating linkers, but the direct connection is lost and re- establishing that connection requires more than a mere disassembler. Especially small constants may have more than one possible name. Operating system calls (like dll's in MS- Windows, or syscalls in Unices) may be reconstructed, as their names appear in a separate segment or are known beforehand. Many disassemblers allow the user to attach a name to a label or constant based on his understanding of the code. These identifiers, in addition to comments in the source file, help to make the code more readable to a human, and can also shed some clues on the purpose of the code. Without these comments and identifiers, it is harder to understand the purpose of the source code, and it can be difficult to determine the algorithm being used by that code. When you combine this problem with the possibility that the code you are trying to read may, in reality, be data (as outlined above), then it can be ever harder to determine what is going on.

## Decompilers

Akin to Disassembly, Decompilers take the process a step further and actually try to reproduce the code in a high level language. Frequently, this high level language is C, because C is simple and primitive enough to facilitate the decompilation process. Decompilation does have its drawbacks, because lots of data and readability constructs are lost during the original compilation process, and they cannot be reproduced. Since the science of decompilation is still young, and results are "good" but not "great", this page will limit itself to a listing of decompilers, and a general (but brief) discussion of the possibilities of decompilation.

### *Tools*

As with other software, embedded system designers use compilers, assemblers, and debuggers to develop embedded system software. However, they may also use some more specific tools:

In circuit debuggers or emulators (see next section).

Utilities to add a checksum or CRC to a program, so the embedded system can check if the program is valid.

For systems using digital signal processing, developers may use a math workbench such as Scilab/Scicos, MATLAB/Simulink, EICASLAB, MathCad, Mathematica, or FlowStone DSP to simulate the mathematics. They might also use libraries for both the host and target which eliminates developing DSP routines as done in DSPnano RTOS.

Model based development tool like VisSim lets you create and simulate graphical data flow and UML State chart diagrams of components like digital filters, motor controllers, communication protocol decoding and multi-rate tasks.

Interrupt handlers can also be created graphically. After simulation, you can automatically generate C-code to the VisSim RTOS which handles the main control task and preemption of background tasks, as well as automatic setup and programming of on-chip peripherals.

Custom compilers and linkers may be used to optimize specialized hardware.

Embedded system may have its own special language or design tool, or add enhancements to an existing language such as Forth or Basic.

Another alternative is to add a real-time operating system or embedded operating system, which may have DSP capabilities like DSPnano RTOS.

Modeling and code generating tools often based on state machines Software tools can come from several sources:

Software companies that specialize in the embedded market Ported from the GNU software development tools

Sometimes, development tools for a personal computer can be used if the embedded processor is a close relative to a common PC processor

As the complexity of embedded systems grows, higher level tools and operating systems are migrating into machinery where it makes sense. For example, cellphones, personal digital assistants and other consumer computers often need significant software that is purchased or provided by a person other than the manufacturer of the electronics. In these systems, an open programming environment such as Linux, NetBSD, OSGi or Embedded Java is required so that the third-party software provider can sell to a large market.

## Debugging

Embedded debugging may be performed at different levels, depending on the facilities available. From simplest to most sophisticated they can be roughly grouped into the following areas:

Interactive resident debugging, using the simple shell provided by the embedded operating system (e.g. Forth and Basic).

External debugging using logging or serial port output to trace operation using either a monitor in flash or using a debug server like the Remedy Debugger which even works for heterogeneous multicore systems.

An in-circuit debugger (ICD), a hardware device that connects to the microprocessor via a JTAG or Nexus interface. This allows the operation of the microprocessor to be controlled externally, but is typically restricted to specific debugging capabilities in the processor. An in-circuit emulator (ICE) replaces the microprocessor with a simulated equivalent, providing full control over all aspects of the microprocessor.

A complete emulator provides a simulation of all aspects of the hardware, allowing all of it to be controlled and modified, and allowing debugging on a normal PC. The downsides are expense and slow operation, in some cases up to 100X slower than the final system. For SoC designs, the typical approach is to verify and debug the design on an FPGA prototype board. Tools such as Certus [8] are used to insert probes in the FPGA RTL that make signals available for observation. This is used to debug hardware, firmware and software interactions across multiple FPGA with capabilities similar to a logic analyzer.

Unless restricted to external debugging, the programmer can typically load and run software through the tools, view the code running in the processor, and start or stop its operation. The view of the code may be as HLL source-code, assembly code or mixture of both.

Because an embedded system is often composed of a wide variety of elements, the debugging strategy may vary. For instance, debugging a software (and microprocessor-) centric embedded system is different from debugging an embedded system where most of the processing is performed by peripherals (DSP, FPGA, co-processor). An increasing number of embedded systems today use more than one single processor core. A common problem with multi-core development is the proper synchronization of software execution. In such a case, the embedded system design may wish to check the data traffic on the busses between the processor cores, which requires very low-level debugging, at signal/bus level, with a logic analyzer, for instance.

Simulation is the imitation of the operation of a real-world process or system over time.[1] The act of simulating something first requires that a model be developed; this model represents the key characteristics or behaviors/functions of the selected physical or abstract system or process. The model represents the system itself, whereas the simulation represents the operation of the system over time. Simulation is used in many contexts, such as simulation of technology for performance optimization, safety engineering, testing, training, education, and video games. Often, computer experiments are used to study simulation models. Simulation is also used with scientific modelling of natural systems or human systems to gain insight into their functioning.[2] Simulation can be used to show the eventual real effects of alternative conditions and courses of action. Simulation is also used when the real system cannot be engaged, because it may not be accessible, or it may be dangerous or unacceptable to engage, or it is being designed but not yet built, or it may simply not exist.[3].

Key issues in simulation include acquisition of valid source information about the relevant selection of key characteristics and behaviours, the use of simplifying approximations and assumptions within the simulation, and fidelity and validity of the simulation outcomes.

## Emulator

This article is about emulators in computing. For a line of digital musical instruments, see E-mu Emulator. For the Transformers character, see Circuit Breaker (Transformers)#Shattered Glass. For other uses, see Emulation (disambiguation).

DOSBox emulates the command-line interface of DOS.

In computing, an emulator is hardware or software or both that duplicates (or emulates) the functions of one computer system (the guest) in another computer system (the host), different from the first one, so that the emulated behavior closely resembles the behavior of the real system (the guest).

The above described focus on exact reproduction of behavior is in contrast to some other forms of computer simulation, in which an abstract model of a system is being simulated. For example, a computer simulation of a hurricane or a chemical reaction is not emulation.

### *Emulation in Preservation*

Emulation is a strategy in digital preservation to combat obsolescence. Emulation focuses on recreating an original computer environment, which can be time-consuming and difficult to achieve, but valuable because of its ability to maintain a closer connection to the authenticity of the digital object.[2]

Emulation addresses the original hardware and software environment of the digital object, and recreates it on a current machine.[3] The emulator allows the user to have access to any kind of application or operating system on a current platform, while the software runs as it did in its original environment.[4] Jeffery Rothenberg, an early proponent of emulation as a digital preservation strategy states, "the ideal approach would provide a single  extensible, long-term solution that can be designed once and for all and applied uniformly,  automatically, and in synchrony (for example, at every refresh cycle) to all types of documents and media".[5] He further states that this should not only apply to out of date systems, but also be upwardly mobile to future unknown systems.[6] Practically speaking, when a certain application is released in a new version, rather than address compatibility issues and migration for every digital object created in the previous version of that application, one could create an emulator for the application, allowing access to all of said digital objects.

### *Benefits*

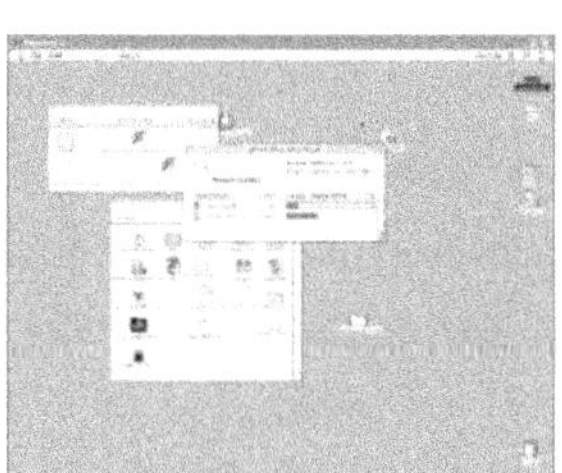

Basilisk II emulates a Macintosh 68k using interpretation code and dynamic recompilation. Potentially better graphics quality than original hardware.

Potentially additional features original hardware didn't have.

Save states.

Emulators allow users to play games for discontinued consoles.

Emulators maintain the original look, feel, and behavior of the digital object, which is just as important as the digital data itself.[7]

Despite the original cost of developing an emulator, it may prove to be the more cost efficient solution over time.[8]

Reduces labor hours, because rather than continuing anongoing task of continual data migration for every digital object, once the library of past and present operating systems and application software is established in an emulator, these same technologies are used for every document using those platforms.[4]

Many emulators have already been developed and released under GNU General Public License through the open source environment, allowing for wide scale collaboration.[9]

Allow software exclusive to one system to be used on another. For example, a PlayStation 2 exclusive video game could (in theory) be played on a PC or Xbox 360 using an emulator. This is especially useful when the original system is difficult to obtain, or incompatible with modern equipment (e.g. old video game consoles which connect via analog outputs may be unable to connect to modern TVs which may only have digital input

Obstacles Intellectual property-Many technology vendors implemented non-standard features during program development in order to establish their niche in the market, while simultaneously applying ongoing upgrades to remain competitive. While this may have advanced the technology industry and increased vendor's market share, it has left users lost in a preservation nightmare with little supporting documentation due to the proprietary nature of the hardware and software. Laws are not yet in effect to address saving the documentation and specifications of proprietary software and hardware in an emulator module.[11]

Emulators are often used as a copyright infringement tool, since they allow users to play video games without having to buy the console, and rarely make any attempt to prevent the use of illegal copies. This leads to a number of legal uncertainties regarding emulation, and leads to software being programmed to refuse to work if it can tell the host is an emulator; some video games in particular will continue to run, but not allow the player to progress beyond some late stage in the game, often appearing to be faulty or just extremely difficult.[12][13] These protections make it more difficult to design emulators, since they must be accurate enough to avoid triggering the protections, whose effects may not be obvious.

### Emulators in new Media Art

Because of its primary use of digital formats, new media art relies heavily on emulation as a preservation strategy.

Artists such as Cory Arcangel specialize in resurrecting obsolete technologies in their artwork and recognize the importance of a decentralized and deinstitutionalized process for the preservation of digital culture.

In many cases, the goal of emulation in new media art is to preserve a digital medium so that it can be saved indefinitely and reproduced without error, so that there is no reliance on hardware that ages and becomes obsolete. The paradox is that the emulation and the emulator have to be made to work on future computers.

### Emulation in Future Systems Design

Emulation technics are commonly used during the design and development of new systems. It eases the development process by providing the ability to detect, recreate and repair flaws in the design even before the system is actually built.[15] It is particularly useful in the design of multi-cores systems, where concurrency errors can be very difficult to detect and correct without the controlled environment provided by virtual hardware.[16]  This also allows the software development to take place before the hardware is ready,[17] thus helping to validate design decisions.

### Structure of An Emulator

Typically, an emulator is divided into modules that correspond roughly to the emulated computer's subsystems. Most often, an emulator will be composed of the following modules:

- A CPU emulator or CPU simulator (the two terms are mostly interchangeable in this case), unless the target being emulated has the same CPU architecture as the host, in which case a virtual machine layer may be used instead
- A memory subsystem module various I/O devices emulators
- Buses are often not emulated, either for reasons of performance or simplicity, and virtual peripherals communicate directly with the CPU or the memory subsystem.

# VTU Question Bank

## Unit-1

1) Give the characteristics and constraint of embedded system?                    Jun 14

2) Explain the challenges in embedded computing system design.

                                                                    Jun 14/Jan 14

3) Define design methodology. Explain the embedded system design process?

                                                                              Jun 14

4) Explain model train control system?

                                                                              Jan 14

5) Discuss the requirements chart with an example

                                                                            Jan 2015

6) Explain the sequence diagram for transmitting control input in modern train controller.

                                                                            Jan 2015

7) Explain the UML class diagram for signal and time out events.

                                                                            Jan 2015

8) Define Embedded System. Explain the embedded system process.

                                                                       June/July 2015

9) Define digital Command control(DCC) Explain the conceptual specification of a model.

                                                                       June/July 2015

10) What is embedded Computing system? Mention its Characteristics.

                                                                             Dec2015

11) Explain embedded system design process with respect to GPS moving Map.

                                                                             Dec2015

12) Draw and explain the sequence diagram for transmitting a control input in a model train controller.

                                                                             Dec2015

13) What is embedded system? Give one example.

                                                                       June/July 2016

14) Explain briefly the characteristics of an embedded computing application.

                                                                       June/July 2016

15) Write the top down view of the embedded system design process and write a requirement chart of model train controller.                    June/July 2016

# Unit-2

1) Differentiate between Harvard and von Neumann architecture.  Jun 14

2) Define ARM processor. Explain advanced ARM features?

Jun 14

3) What is pipelining? Explain the c55X of a seven stages of pipeline with a neat diagram of ARM instructions?

Jun 14/Jan 14

4) Explain memory system mechanisms?

Jan 14

5) What are interrupts? Discuss its mechanism, with a neatdiagram.

Jan 2015

6) Draw the format of ARM data processing instructions

Jan 2015

7) What is associative cache? Explain.

Jan 2015

8) Explain the various data operations in ARM.

June/July 2015

9) Explain in detail the programming of I/O devices

June/July 2015

10) Write ARM assembly code to implement the following Cassignments

i)x=(a-b)+(c*d)

ii) y=(a<<3)|(b&1b)

Dec2015

11) Explain the pipelined execution of a branch in ARM using a pipelinediagram. Dec2015

12) What is cache? Explain the following with diagram

   i)       Two level Cache

   ii)      direct mapped cache

   iii)     Set Associative Cache

13) Write ARM assembly code to implement the following C assignment. Z=a(b+c)-d*e

June/July 2016

14) What is an interrupt priorities mechanismused to handle multiple devices interrupts?

June/July 2016

15) What is cache? How it relates to memory system mechanism? Explain different types of cache miss.  June/July 2016

# Unit-3

1) Write the major components of bus protocol. Explain the burst read transaction with a neat timing diagram?

Jun 14/Jan 14

2) Describe: i) Timer ii) cross compiler iii) logic analyzer         Jan 14

3) Explain the glue logic interface?

Jun 14

4) Explain components of embedded programs?

Jun 14

5) Explain the bus with DMA controller.

Jan 2015

6) Justify PC as a platform for embedded system

Jan 2015

7) Briefly discuss the process of two stage address translation in ARM

Jan 2015

8) Discuss memory interfacing and I/O interfacing in brief.

June/July 2015

9) What is DMA? Explain with the neat diagram

June/July 2015

10) Explain briefly the development and debugging of an alarm clock.

June/July 2015

11) Draw a UML state diagram of the bus bridge operation and explain.

Dec 2015

12) Explain with a neat diagram, the bus with a DMA Controller.

Dec 2015

13) Write the requirement Table for Alarm Clock.

Dec 2015

14) Explain a bus with a DMA controller mechanism?

June/July 2016

15) Differentiate between Random accesses memories and read only memories.

June/July 2016

16) List out the I/O devices commonly used in embedded computing system. Explain briefly any three I/O devices.

June/July 2016

## Unit-4

1) Write a note on DMA controller?                                          Jan 14

2) Explain the circular buffers for embedded programs?

                                                                      Jun14/Jan 14

3) With a neat sketch, explain the role of assemblers and linkers in compilation process.

                                                                            Jun 14

4) Explain with example techniques in optimizing.

                                                                      Jun 14/Jan 14

5) Sketch and explain the data flow graph model

                                                                          Jan 2015

6) Explain the program optimization techniques.

                                                                          Jan 2015

7) Explain the data flow and control/data flow graphs for programming models.

                                                                      June/July 2015

8) List and explain different program optimization techniques.

                                                                      June/July 2015

9) Briefly Explain Control/Data floe graphs. Draw the CDFG for the C code given below.

                                                                          Dec2015

10) Show the contents table of the assemblers symbol table at the end of code generatio for each line of the following program:

    Org 100
    P1 CMP r0,r1
    Beq p1 p2 cmp r0,r2 BEQ P2
    P3 CMP R0,R3
    BEQ P3

                                                                          Dec2015

11) Explain briefly different types of peerformance measures on programs.        Dec2015

12) For a given basic Block, rewrite it in single assignment form and then draw the data flow graph.

    W=a+b X=a-c
    Y=x+d X=a+c F=y+e

                                                                      June/July 2016

13) Explain any two program optimization techniques.

                                                                      June/July 2016

14) Write a short note on alarm clocks.

                                                                      June/July 2016

# Unit-5

1) Explain operating system Architecture, with a neat diagram?

Jan 14

2) Define different types of operating system?

Jan 14

3) What is RTOS? List and explain the different services of RTOS.

Jun 14

4) Describe the concept of multithreading and write the comparison between thread and process.

Jun 14

5) What is TCB? Explain its structure

Jan 2015

6) Explain the structure of process.

Jan 2015

7) What is multi-processing? Explain its types.

Jan 2015

8) What are the factors considered for selection of scheduling algorithm?

Jan 2015

9) With the neat diagram , Explain RTOS Architecture.

June/July 2015

10) Define the following:

June/July 2015

   i)Task

   ii)Deadlock

   iii)Semaphore

   iv)Scheduler

   v) Remote procedure call (RPC)

11) Explain how threads and processes are used in RTOS.

June/July 2015

12) What is real time operating system and real time kernel? Define Task Control Block (TCB) and describe the structure of a TCB.

Dec2015

13) Explain the synchronization issues in resource allocation using the Dining Philosophers Problem. Mention the solutions for those issues.

Dec2015

14) Explain the basic function of real time Kernel.

June/July 2016

15) Give difference between monolithic kernel and micro kernel.

June/July 2016

16) Define process. With a diagram, explain state transition of a process.

June/July 2016

# Unit-6

1) Define blocking and non blocking communication. Explain the two styles of interposes communication, with a example.

Jun 14

2) What are the assumptions for the performance of a real system running process? Mention the factors affect context switching time and interrupt latency.

Jun 14/Jan 14

3) Explain shared memory communication implemented on a bus?

Jan 14

4) Explain the technique in shared memory communication

Jan 2014

5) Explain the following:

   i)   L-shaped usage distribution

Jan 2015

6) Explain the technique in shared memory communication.

Jan 2015

7) Explain the following:

   i.   L-shaped usage distribution

Jan 2015

8) Explain Inter-process communication and synchronization with signals

June/July 2015

9) List the different functional and non-functional requirements while choosing anRTOS.

June/July 2015

10) Explain Briefly the concept of counting Semaphores andmutex.

Dec2015

11) What is advanced configuration and power interface? Erxplain the basic global power states supported by ACPI.

Dec2015

12) Describe hoe to evaluate OS performance in terms of the following:     Dec2015

   1)   Context Switching

   2)   Cache Scheduling

13) What is Inter process communication (IPC)? Give an overview of different types of IPC mechanisms adapted by various operating systems.

June/July 2016

14) What is deadlock? What are the different conditions favoringdeadlock?

June/July 2016

15) Explain the different functional requirements that need to be evaluated in the selection of an RTOS.

June/July 2016

# Unit-7

1) Explain hardware and software Architecture of distributed embedded system?

Jan 14

2) Explain about multichip communication with a neat diagram?

Jan 14

3) With a neat sketch, explain the CAN data frame format and typical bus transactions on the IC bus.

Jun 14

4) Explain Ethernet format and IP structure.

Jun 14

5) Explain the $I^2C$ bus

Jan 2015

6) What is multi Hop communication?

Jan 2015

7) Explain the structure of IP packets

Jan 2015

8) Discuss any one application of internet

Jan 2015

9) Define a distributed embedded system .Explain.

June/July 2015

10) Compare $I^2C$ bus and CAN bus over their use in embedded system.

June/July 2015

11) Describe the requirements for elevator Controller in brief.

June/July 2015

12) With the neat diagram, Explain the various fields of CAN Frame.

Dec2015

13) Explain a neat diagram , the structure of an IP packet

Dec2015

14) Explain the structure and characteristics of an I2C bus.

June/July 2016

15) Explain Ethernet packet format.

June/July 2016

16) explain the following terms June/July   2016

# Unit-8

1) Write a note on object file and map file.

Jan 14

2) Explain about simulators, emulators and debuggers.

Jan 14

3) What is simulator? Explain its features.

Jun 14

4) What are the improvements over firmware software debugging? Explain

Jun 14

5) What is a simulator? Explain its advantages and limitations

Jan 2015

6) What is boundary scan? Explain

Jan 2015

7) What is monitor program based firmware debugging

Jan 2015

8) Write short notes on

a) IDE

b) Pre-emptive Scheduler.

C) Simulator and Emulator

D) Target System

June/July 2015

9) With the neat diagram, Explain elements of the ARM AMBA bus system.

Dec2015

10) Write the short notes on Logic Analyzer.

Dec2015

11) Explain with a diagram the concept of context switching, context saving and context retrieval

Dec2015

12) Difference between Non preemptive SJF scheduling algorithm and preemptive SJF scheduling algorithm with simple examples

Dec2015

13) Explain the following interacted development Environment

June/July 2016

14) Explain the different tools used for hardware debugging.                    June/July 2016